Grant—

You are a

Game-Changer!

Jimmy Page

To:

From:

Date:

What People Are Saying About *WisdomWalks SPORTS*

A game plan for anyone who wants to grow in Christ, written by men who have done just that!

> KYLE ROTE JR., 2010 Soccer Hall of Fame, ESPN's "Greatest All-Around Athlete" of All Time, national commentator for CBS, PBS, and USA Cable

Whether you're in the locker room, the board room, or the living room, if you're intentional about walking like Jesus, you will influence people. *WisdomWalks* gives you **a winning game plan** to invest biblical truth in the lives of others.

> MATT STOVER, twenty-year NFL player for the Baltimore Ravens, Indianapolis Colts, Cleveland Browns, and New York Giants

A great resource for parents, coaches, and anyone who cares about kids and their futures.

> LES STECKEL, president/CEO of the Fellowship of Christian Athletes and twenty-two-year NFL coach

A very **useful, practical field guide** based upon forty biblical principles that get one to "true north." Packed with practical wisdom and eternal truths.

> TOM OSBORNE, athletic director of the University of Nebraska, former twenty-five-year head coach of the Huskers, and author of *More Than Winning*

LIVE INTENTIONALLY.
MAXIMIZE RELATIONSHIPS. PASS THE TORCH.

40 GAME-CHANGING PRINCIPLES
FOR ATHLETES, COACHES & TEAMS

DAN BRITTON AND JIMMY PAGE

summerside
PRESS™

DEDICATION

*To all the coaches and athletes who are walking with Jesus,
investing in others, and changing the world.*

Summerside Press™
Minneapolis, MN 55378
www.summersidepress.com
WisdomWalks SPORTS
© 2012 by Dan Britton and Jimmy Page

ISBN 978-1-60936-684-1

Stock or custom editions of Summerside Press titles may be purchased in bulk for educational,
business, ministry, fundraising, or sales promotional use.
For information, please e-mail specialmarkets@summersidepress.com

Cover design by Chris Gilbert, Studio Gearbox
Interior design and typesetting by Jeff Jansen

Slipcase photo of rowers by Getty Images; other slipcase photos by Dan Michael Hodges.
Author photos © 2010 by Dan Michael Hodges

*Summerside Press™ is an inspirational publisher offering fresh,
irresistible books to uplift the heart and engage the mind.*

Printed in China

EXERCISE WISDOM

Do you not know that in a race all the runners run, but only one receives the prize? So run that you may obtain it.... I do not run aimlessly; I do not box as one beating the air. But I discipline my body and keep it under control.

1 Corinthians 9:24, 26–27 ESV

The world of sports is not just a phenomenon that has been brought to our generation in recent years. In fact, sport is as old as the Bible itself. When the Apostle Paul talked about "running the race," he was thinking about the Olympic games that were held in Delphi, Olympus, and played in the Parthenon. When he said, "I discipline my body," he was referring to athletes who trained for those games. The Bible talks about sports, and in those days chariot races, boxing, and even track events were all part of that world. When an athlete won the gold he was honored in several ways. A statue was erected in his honor. Songs were written that would give national acclaim to the athlete and his family. Athletes were even known to be exempt from paying taxes to Rome for the rest of their lives. Cicero said athletes in his day received greater fame and honor than conquering generals who returned from victory.

Interesting isn't it? Not much has changed. Athletes are still idolized, held in high esteem, and many times put on pedestals too high for anyone to reach. If there is anything athletes, coaches, teams, and the entire industry of sports need today, it is a healthy dose of God's wisdom.

James tells us "the wisdom from above is first pure, then peaceable, gentle, open to reason, full of mercy and good fruits, impartial and sincere" (James 3:17 ESV). If you are a coach, athlete, or just love to watch sports, you need to play and walk with that kind of wisdom in every aspect of your life to be a winner on and off the field. What Dan Britton and Jimmy Page have written with *WisdomWalks SPORTS* is more than a book—it's a guide with forty principles that can be not only game changers but life changers too.

As an athlete and coach, I can tell you the team is all about relationships. This book is a great blend of mentoring, maturing, and managing your life for impact. I was blessed as a young athlete not only with great coaches but also with a wise mom and dad who taught wisdom principles that are still making their difference today. In addition to teaching those principles, they lived them out and modeled them every day.

Today my team consists primarily of my family, and believe me, they treasure that wisdom as much as anyone on the playing field. Every team needs a playbook. Every coach needs a game plan. Every athlete who wants to be a difference maker and a game changer needs wisdom. What you're holding in your hands is a playbook and plan not only for your game but for your life. So as you read it, enjoy your walk. And whatever your sport, exercise wisdom. It really will be the difference in your game.

Tony Dungy

WISDOMWALKS SPORTS GAME PLAN

Get ready.
It's game time.

Watch your step. Use your head. Make the most of every chance you get.
These are desperate times! Don't live carelessly, unthinkingly.
Make sure you understand what the Master wants.

EPHESIANS 5:16-17 MSG

Not long ago I saw an athlete in the gym wearing a T-shirt with the saying "No Pain—No Pain." It was obviously a play on the old adage "No Pain—No Gain." I watched him for thirty minutes while I ran on the treadmill. This guy was truly living out his shirt, just talking to the ladies and visiting with the gym staff. There wasn't a drop of sweat on him. It goes to show that the world values shortcuts as the key to success. The easy way becomes the best way—not hard work and unwavering discipline.

Many competitors live with the "No Pain—No Pain" (NP²) mind-set and never fulfill their God-given potential. They waste the gift. There is no progress without struggle. There is no growth unless we push beyond our normal limits. Many competitors want the win without the work. But the shortcut never leads to greatness. The easy road never makes you better.

Often we carry the NP² mind-set right into our spiritual lives. While there's nothing we can do to earn eternal life and no amount of effort earns us a place in heaven, once we're born again, the ongoing transformation process requires daily surrendering of ourselves and a supernatural work of God. When the gospel is presented as merely a quick prayer to add Jesus to someone's life, we see the NP² gospel at work. Just plug Jesus in, and He'll make your life so much better. No change, no sacrifice, no confession of sin, no pain, no sweat, no effort, no surrender. NP² Jesus will give you peace and purpose, if you add Him to your already well-planned-out life…right?

But don't buy into the spiritual NP^2 trap. If Jesus Christ becomes the Lord and Savior of your life, you can continue in the same direction, but why on earth would you? What a waste that would be. Jesus gives us a choice. His great love and sacrifice compel us to walk a different path, to go against the flow, and to be set apart. When you believe in Jesus and He gives you new life, you will do a total redirect, a 180-degree turn, saying, "God, I give up control of my life to You. It's YOUR plan, not my plan; Your way, not my way."

But it's hard to give up control of our lives, isn't it? Even to the God of the universe. We find it difficult and painful to let God make us into the men and women He destined us to be. Change comes hard, and it hurts. So we take the easy road in our spiritual lives. The NP^2 spiritual life is easy—no spiritual sweat, no digging into deep spiritual truths, no seeking after what pleases God, no discipline. Unfortunately, the same disciplines that make us successful on the field of competition as athletes and coaches are not applied to our spiritual lives.

Just imagine if your sports team's success was built on your devotion to Christ rather than your skills, your talents, your training, your discipline, the team's game plan, and coaching staff. Would your team have a winning record? Or would you be struggling in last place in the conference?

Christ desires to take control of our lives—and He does a far better job. But be forewarned: your life will not stay the same. God loves you so much that He says, "Come as you are." But He also loves you too much to leave you in that condition. His goal is forgiveness, freedom, and fruit in the life of the believer. In Luke 9:23, Jesus says, "If anyone would come after me, he must deny himself and take up his cross daily and follow me." But the results are so worth it!

God is waiting to transform you. He wants one-on-one time with you. He doesn't want to become a key part of your life. Instead, He wants to *become your life.*

That's where *WisdomWalks SPORTS* comes in. It's a tool to energize and transform your life as an athlete, coach, or teammate. We believe when competitors are transformed, they will transform the way sports are coached, played, and even watched. It's our vision to see the world of sports redeemed for Christ. The platform of sport is arguably the largest and most influential platform in the world; the language of sport transcends gender, race, age, and even nationality. Sport is truly the international language.

As athletes and coaches, when you live intentionally, maximize relationships, and pass the torch, you become difference makers. You grow increasingly passionate about life and excited about relationships, and your desire to understand and know God is amped up. You realize your faith isn't something you leave on the sidelines. You are a player, not a fan! Instead, it helps define every aspect of who you are and how you compete. You're not a Christian competitor; you are a Christian who competes. Who you are in Christ comes with you to the field. Your identity is in Christ, not in your sport. It doesn't depend on your last performance or your win-loss record.

WisdomWalks Is Not a Play; It's a *Playbook*.

Anybody can make a big play. But living an authentic, consistent life for Christ takes persistence and perseverance. It's not a "one and done"; it's a strategy for winning. It's a practical playbook with key principles every competitor needs for peak performance, both on the field and off. Best of all, it's based on the ultimate playbook—the Bible.

WisdomWalks Is Not a Result; It's a *Relationship*.

This is not about achieving a goal. It's not a scoreboard that tallies wins and losses. It's not something you check off your to-do list. Instead, it's about relationships. It's about intentionally investing your life in getting to know God more, and then investing in the lives of others to impact your teammates, athletes, and coaches.

WisdomWalks Is Not a Moment; It's a *Movement*.

This is not about crossing a finish line or hitting a buzzer-beater. It's about creating personal, spiritual momentum that begins to change the very culture of competition—from the gym to the locker room to the field. WisdomWalkers elevate the perspective and performance of everyone around them. Spiritual momentum spreads to your team, campus, and community. It fosters belief and trust and creates an uncommon unity and focus. Ultimately, it can transform the world of sports.

Understanding who we are in Christ is a game changer:

And now, just as you accepted Christ Jesus as your Lord, you must continue to follow him. Let your roots grow down into him, and let your lives be built on him. Then your faith will grow strong in the truth you were taught, and you will overflow with thankfulness.

COLOSSIANS 2:6-7 (NLT)

Becoming a WisdomWalker means walking with Jesus in *everything*—on the field, at home, at school, at church, in the locker room. And that identity in Christ completely changes your mind and heart until you realize that everything you have comes from God. Every time you step onto the field of competition your heart explodes with thankfulness, because you are abundantly grateful for God's blessings. You have a deep conviction that your gifts, talents, and skills to play and to compete come from Him alone. And you never take them for granted. Every stride, swing, shot, pass, goal, and point is a response of gratitude for God's goodness.

In competition, it's easy to give God thanks when everything goes our way. When we score the touchdown or hit the home run or finish first, it's easy to praise Him. But what about when we experience adversity or heartbreak? How do we respond then? Is our gratitude dependent on our circumstances or performance? Or will we look for God to turn our trials into testimonies? Do we seek God for what we can get from Him? Or do we seek Him to find Him alone?

If we only seek Him and thank Him for what He does, we will end up disillusioned and disappointed when He doesn't do what we want Him to. God is not a lucky charm or a rabbit's foot. He desires that we seek Him simply to know Him.

WisdomWalks SPORTS is about putting God first in every area. It means being thankful for *who* He is, not for *what* He can do for us.

With a grateful heart, much can be accomplished. So let the competition begin!

DAN BRITTON and JIMMY PAGE

BUILD YOUR DREAM TEAM

Choose your team wisely.
Teammates will make or break you.

The "Dream Team" was the nickname given to the 1992 United States men's Olympic basketball team. It was the first American Olympic team to feature active NBA players, and the results were awesome. As they dominated their way to the gold medal, they beat their opponents by an average of forty-four points! Since the Dream Team, the United States has had numerous teams with the best and most talented players, but USA basketball has never been able to repeat the Dream Team's success.

We always think the best team consists of the best players. However, the best team is about getting the right players. In the movie *Miracle*, US Olympic hockey coach Herb Brooks has a classic line when he is selecting the 1980 team. He shows the roster of players who will be a part of the team to his assistant coach, Craig Patrick. Shocked at who is on the list, Craig says, "You're missing some of the best players." Coach Brooks responds, "I'm not looking for the best players, Craig. I'm looking for the right ones."

If you could assemble your own Dream Team, who would be on it? We're not talking about a sports team, but your own team of godly friends who build you up when you're down, pick you up when you stumble, guide you when you're uncertain, and confront you when you're out of bounds. We all need a few steadfast friends to do life with. Who are the right teammates to ensure your personal and spiritual success? Who will be in your "inner circle," walking with you through thick and thin, pouring God's wisdom into your mind and heart?

Building your Dream Team is what *WisdomWalks* is about. Getting the right people on your team and understanding the role they play is essential. Life gets complicated quickly, and without those key people, it can get overwhelming. When we go with the flow, we drift toward complexity. However, when we are intentional, we drive toward clarity. *WisdomWalks* helps you create relational clarity by defining these relationships.

A WisdomWalker's Dream Team has four key relationships: Walker, Watchman, Warrior, and Workman. It's the perfect blend of mentoring, accountability, and discipleship. Without these key relationships, it will be increasingly more difficult for you to live a life that matters—a life of influence. We need an inner circle that brings us to Jesus, because in Christ is the fullness of wisdom.

> *Christ is the power of God and the wisdom of God. This foolish plan of God is wiser than the wisest of human plans, and God's weakness is stronger than the greatest of human strength.*
>
> 1 Corinthians 1:24–25 NLT

All you need to become a WisdomWalker is to have the personal desire and the practical discipline to walk like Jesus and make a difference in the lives of those you care about. You can be a catalyst for generational change by investing in others! Ultimately, the fruit of a WisdomWalker grows on other people's trees.

We have developed a simple formula for WisdomWalks:

Wisdom – Relationships = Nothing

No matter how much godly wisdom you have, unless it is infused into relationships, it's worth nothing. The power of wisdom is not quantity but context. As we grow in Christ, there should be a natural growing of our relationships, because our God is a relational God. As godly wisdom increases, relationships become richer and fuller. There is always a direct connection between wisdom and relationships.

Wisdom + Relationships = Influence

However, when the wisdom of Jesus is applied in our relationships, we experience two-way influence. Influence is God's work though us. It establishes an eternal legacy. But wisdom is only valuable if it's lived out in relationships. Life is a team sport. We must assemble our own Dream Team with an inner circle of people whose singular goal, in everything they become and do, is for God's glory. If you want to experience transformation in your life and relationships, it all begins with the Wisdom

Walks journey...and the four key relationships (for more, see "The Four Relationships" on pp. 9–10).

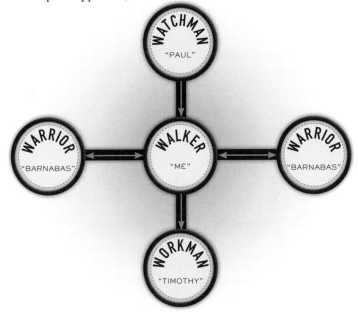

Life is all about relationships.

Proverbs 18:1 (HCSB) says, "One who isolates himself pursues selfish desires; he rebels against all sound judgment." In other words, we make foolish decisions. Isolation is the silent enemy. If we distance ourselves from relationships, we will crash and burn. Most people float along and never take the time to develop a Dream Team.

Each one of us needs to be a Walker, have a Watchman, have a Warrior, and have a Workman. The WisdomWalks journey is multidimensional. On a team, you have teammates and you are a teammate. Once you get your Dream Team assembled, you will realize the full power of WisdomWalks: every Walker not only has these key relationships in his or her life but also plays these roles for others. You have a Warrior, and you are a Warrior. You have a Watchman, and you are a Watchman. You have a Workman, and you are Workman. And all of you are Walkers.

In order to help you recruit the right teammates, we've provided the image below. It is blank so that you can fill in names in each circle. Your name goes in the middle. It's okay to have one or two empty circles; it just means you have some work to do. You need to pray and wait, but also search and ask. Make sure you define the relationship. *WisdomWalks* is not about connecting with people once a week for a meal or cup of coffee without a clear purpose for growth.

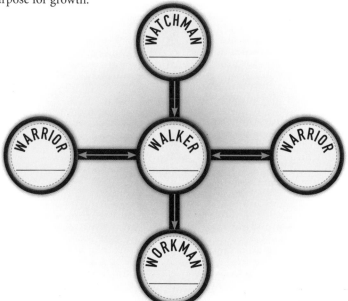

Ask God to reveal to you who needs to join your Dream Team. There are people already in your life who are ready and able, so start recruiting the right teammates. You'll be amazed as you and every other WisdomWalker on your Dream Team begin to live out a passionate, unstoppable faith in Jesus Christ—both on and off the field.

Get ready for a *WisdomWalks* experience so powerful it'll transform your life, your team, your coaches, and generations to come. It's time to get in the game!

Live Intentionally. Maximize Relationships. Pass the Torch.

THE FOUR RELATIONSHIPS

The Walker

The *Walker* is you. This relationship is your own passionate pursuit of Jesus. So before you try to start identifying significant people in your life and what role they possibly can play, take the *WisdomWalks* journey yourself. First John 2:6 says, "Whoever claims to live in him must walk as Jesus did." This biblical challenge encourages us to grow spiritually first. You can't give away what you don't have. Your public impact on others is directly related to your private walk with Jesus.

A Walker does two things—*pursues* and *abides*. Pursuing is engaging God daily, no matter what. The Walker will connect with almighty God each day, understanding that the most vital part of the day is time spent before God in worship and study. Abiding is the sustaining, day-to-day walking with Jesus. We all need to be Walkers, and we need other Walkers in our life to help us pursue and abide. Are you a Walker?

The Walker: •Engages God daily. •Reads and meditates on the Word.
•Prays and listens. •Worships and pursues.

The Warrior

The *Warrior* is a close friend. There is mutual mentoring and accountability, with each person completely committed to helping the other become everything God intends. Attitudes and actions are confronted firmly and lovingly. There are no out-of-bounds areas. Proverbs 27:17 says, "As iron sharpens iron, so one man sharpens another." There's transparency that allows real transformation to happen. Warriors form your inner circle of friends.

A Warrior *challenges* and *encourages*. Challenging is the sharpening that takes place through asking the tough questions and making sure there is nothing below the waterline that will sink your life. Every area of life is open for discussion because there is full access. Encouraging others to be authentic is rooted in a desire to see others succeed. Locking up with one or two warriors will radically alter your life. Warriors are go-to teammates on your Dream Team who love you and believe the best in you. When you have a Warrior, you become their Warrior as well. Do you have a Warrior or two?

The Warrior: •Asks the tough questions. •Confronts attitudes and actions.
•Lifts and builds up. •Prevents wandering and drifting.

The Watchman

The *Watchman* is a mentor—a wise teacher who has more life experience and desires to pass on in-the-trenches, real-life wisdom to you, the next generation. Life is all about surrounding yourself with the right people. Proverbs 13:20 (hcsb) says, "The one who walks with the wise will become wise, but a companion of fools will suffer harm." You have the opportunity to capitalize on what the mentor has learned, avoid similar mistakes, and implement proven principles and practices.

A Watchman *guides* and *directs*, because that person is in a different season of life that allows him or her to invest in your future. A Watchman guides by watering the seeds of greatness with opportunities and fertilizing them with encouragement. With constant evaluation of progress, the Watchman can warn you of potential dangers in your life and direct you through God's Word. A Watchman is like a veteran coach on your Dream Team. When you have a Watchman, you become their Workman. Do you have a Watchman?

The Watchman: •Pours out what God has poured in. •Shares life experiences. •Applies the Word to circumstances. •Helps navigate life.

The Workman

The *Workman* is a disciple—someone who has a desire to grow in spiritual maturity and live out the faith. More than a teacher-student relationship, it follows Jesus' model: He lived out the truth and taught it at the same time. In Luke 6:40, Jesus said, "A student is not above his teacher, but everyone who is fully trained will be like his teacher."

A Workman *studies* and *trains* because of an internal passion to grow spiritually. The focus is on discipleship: spiritual training and growth, and using the study and application of God's Word in every area of life. The Workman is the rookie on the Dream Team who has a ton of potential, and your investment will pay big dividends. When you have a Workman, you become their Watchman. Do you have a Workman?

The Workman: •Follows the training plan. •Asks questions, listens, prepares. •Puts wisdom into practice. •Shows honor and appreciation.

THE WISDOMWALKS
COMPETITOR'S CHALLENGE

Live Intentionally. Maximize Relationships. Pass the Torch.

I t's time to take the *WisdomWalks* Competitor's Challenge and start training camp today. Making this commitment to be a WisdomWalker will transform you into a Christ-centered, supernaturally powered difference maker—as a competitor on the field, in the locker room, and in life.

Lord Jesus, I am responding to the call on my life to be a WisdomWalker. I want to be transformed more and more into Your likeness so I can be used to influence my team, coaches, and even the world of sports. And I know I need help in order to become the person You have designed me to be.

As a WisdomWalker:

- I commit to being a Walker.
  I will pursue a personal, passionate relationship with Jesus.
- I commit to having a Warrior or two.
  I will have relationships where iron sharpens iron.
- I commit to having a Watchman.
  I will submit to mentoring from a wise, godly teacher.
- I commit to having a Workman.
  I will invest in the spiritual training of another.

**On this day, I take the Competitor's Challenge
and commit to be a WisdomWalker.**

Signature   Date

Be a WisdomWalker online. *SIGN UP NOW* at www.wisdomwalks.org.

SCAN now for your *free* Weekly Dose of Wisdom!

Whoever claims to live in him
must walk as Jesus did.
1 JOHN 2:6

THE ULTIMATE GAME CHANGER

WisdomWalks Principle
In a single moment, God can change a heart.

*Create a moment for life-change,
and God can change any life in a moment.*
STEVE FITZHUGH

In 1956, as a sophomore lacrosse player at the Naval Academy in Annapolis, Maryland, my dad made a game-changing play. The Midshipmen were up against the Syracuse University Orangemen. Jim Brown, who played for the Orangemen, was not only a standout lacrosse player, but one of the greatest football players ever to play the game. The Orangemen were whipping up on the Midshipmen, and my dad's coach, William "Dinty" Moore, told him to go into the game and make sure Jim Brown was stopped.

A few plays later, my dad saw his opportunity. With Jim Brown running toward him with his head turned the other way to catch the ball, my dad knew this was his moment. Running full speed, he knocked Jim Brown into the scorer's table. Bodies flew everywhere, and the scorer's table was knocked over. As a result of the hit, the Midshipmen were inspired, and they came back and won the game. My dad started every game after that game-changing play.

Game-changing plays have a huge impact on sports history. Some would say those moments are why we watch and play sports.

But spiritual game changers are even more important. The ultimate game changer is the moment we surrender our lives to a living God. This moment, when we place our faith and trust in Jesus Christ and ask Him to be the Lord of our lives, alters everything. He grips our lives in such a way that we take a 180 turn—not just a tweak or slight correction, but a complete turnaround.

Acts 2:38–39 talks about this ultimate game-changing play:

Repent and be baptized, every one of you, in the name of Jesus Christ for the forgiveness of your sins. And you will receive the gift of the Holy Spirit. The promise is for you and your children and for all who are far off—for all whom the Lord our God will call.

Jimmy and I have both experienced this ultimate game-changing play, though our stories are very different.

My spiritual shift happened during the summer of 1975, when I was eight and my mom was leading a Good News Bible Club for the neighborhood kids. With a simple prayer, I asked Jesus to forgive me of my sins and told Him that I wanted to become His child.

However, it was not until July 22, 1982, at a Word of Life summer camp in Schroon Lake, New York, that I completely surrendered everything in my life to Jesus. To symbolize my decision, I threw a woodchip, representing my life, into a bonfire. With tears streaming down my face as a fourteen-year-old, I now understood that prayer I'd prayed with my mom at age eight.

Since then life has never been the same. I still have the little yellow card I signed that evening at camp that says: *All I am, all I have, and all I ever hope to be, I now and forever dedicate to the Lord Jesus Christ for His use and glory, absolutely, unconditionally, now and forever.* The way I lived my life and competed in my sport changed that evening.

Jimmy's ultimate game-changing moment came in college. Here's his story, in his own words:

"I had grown up in a somewhat religious home and had a strong moral compass. I knew right from wrong and did my best to do the right thing because I was a 'pleaser.' I had a great childhood and a great family.

"My dad was a leader in the community, coached my baseball teams, and was well respected. But at home, something changed when alcohol entered the equation. I quickly discovered that the way to please my dad was through performance. So I pursued and found success in both academics and athletics. In my heart, performance became not only my way to earn my dad's love, but my response to my emptiness; it also defined how I related to God. I found that achievement in sports and school brought praise, acceptance, and love.

"But in the end, my pursuit of my father's love, and God's, wore me out. I was only as good as my last game or grade. I was striving for perfection to earn God's favor and avoid the *guilt*. And that burden got heavy to the point that I couldn't carry it anymore. I was tired of trying to earn it, and failing.

"Before I left for college, I saw a radical change in my brother John; he had an unusual peace and was able to weather the verbal pressure from our dad. And I witnessed him reading his Bible for the first time ever. Then at Virginia Tech, I was surrounded by believers who seemed to have what I was looking for—joy, love, forgiveness, and peace. Jesus said, 'Come to me, all you who are weary and burdened, and I will give you rest' (Matthew 11:28). I replaced my religion with relationship. And I dropped my burden for belief. I realized that there was nothing I could do to earn God's love; I would never be good enough. I surrendered my effort and received the life-giving gift of Jesus. I was finally free. 'So if the Son sets you free, you will be free indeed' (John 8:36)."

In John 1:12, Jesus said, "But to all who did receive Him, He gave them the right to be children of God, to those who believe in His name" (HCSB). The spiritual shift took place for each of us, and we both understood Ephesians 2:8–9: "For it is by grace you have been saved, through faith—and this not from yourselves, it is the gift of God—not by works, so that no one can boast." In Romans 10:9–10 (NLT, 2007), Paul calls the game-changing play that brings victory every time:

If you confess with your mouth that Jesus is Lord and believe in your heart that God raised him from the dead, you will be saved. For it is by believing in your heart that you are made right with God, and it is by confessing with your mouth that you are saved.

Have you experienced that spiritual shift in your life? Is there a moment in time that you called on the name of Jesus? If not, today can be your day. In Fellowship of Christian Athletes, we encourage athletes and coaches to pray a prayer of surrender. This prayer is just an expression of what the Lord is doing in your heart. If you would like to trust in Jesus now, here is a prayer we recommend:

"Lord Jesus, I believe. I know there is nothing I can do to earn Your love or to be good enough. I need You. I realize I'm a sinner, and I can't save myself. I need Your forgiveness. I believe You loved me so much that You died on the cross for my sins and rose from the dead. I am sorry for my sins and put my faith in You as Savior and Lord. Today, I surrender my life. I am all in, Jesus. Take control and help me follow You in obedience. I love You, Jesus. In Your name, amen."

Have you prayed this ultimate game-changing prayer? If not, today's the day!

Be a GameChanger!

Live Intentionally. Maximize Relationships. Pass the Torch.

Live It

What are your favorite sports game changers? How did they change the outcome of the game? The life and/or career of the player?

Have you experienced a spiritual game-changing moment? Have you surrendered your life to Christ? If so, when was it, and what happened?

Read Romans 3:10, 23; 5:8, 12; 6:23; 10:9–11, 13. What do these portions of Scripture say about God's plan of salvation? Take some time to thank Jesus for being the Ultimate Game Changer.

Maximize It

Oswald Chambers wrote, "You will never cease to be the most amazed person on earth at what God has done for you on the inside." What has God done for you on the inside?

Read John 10:10. Why is this verse a game changer? Why do most people think having a relationship with Jesus is negative?

Read 2 Corinthians 5:20. What does it mean to be ambassadors for Christ? In what ways can you share Jesus with your team or coaches?

Pass It

Grab a teammate and discuss the *WisdomWalks* principle: *In a single moment, God can change a heart.* Ask, "Have you experienced a spiritual shift in your life?" Share your story of transformation. Pray together for every teammate and coach on your team to make such a game-changing life decision. Use "My GamePlan" below to write the story of your own spiritual game changer.

My GamePlan

_____

_____

_____

_____

_____

_____

_____

_____

_____

_____

_____

_____

_____

_____

_____

_____

_____

_____

Father God, thank You for sending Your Son, Jesus, to die on the cross for me. I am eternally grateful for the love and grace You have poured out. I love You and want to follow and obey You the rest of my life. Help me be the person and the competitor who will give You honor and glory in all I do. My life has changed because of Your love for me. I now know that the Ultimate Game Changer is Jesus Christ! Thank You for transforming my heart. This spiritual shift has changed everything. In Jesus' name, amen.

2

BIGGER. FASTER. STRONGER.

WisdomWalks Principle
We do the training; God does the changing.

*It was character that got us out of bed in the morning,
commitment that moved us into action,
and discipline that enabled us to follow through.*

ZIG ZIGLAR

Growing up, sports were my life. No matter the season, I had a ball in my hand. From football to basketball to baseball, I never let up. We would play pickup games in the neighborhood until dark most days and only head home when one of our moms yelled that dinner was ready. I would even shovel snow from my driveway so I could practice my shooting during the winter. My neighbors would beg me to "go to bed!" because they could hear the ball bouncing late into the night as I played using the dim light from the light post across the street.

When I got to high school, I realized I had to train in a different way to make the teams. I needed to get bigger, stronger, and faster. So my brother and I got a membership at the Nautilus Health Club, and a personal trainer would be waiting to punish us three or four times a week to make us better. And trust me, it worked.

Over 95 percent of an athlete's time is spent training and less than 5 percent competing.

If you want to compete, you have to train. As a sports performance coach, I see athletes work hard year round, in season and out, to prepare their bodies for sport. Coaches develop a training plan, and athletes follow the plan. They make sacrifices to get better. The vast majority of their time is spent on the practice field or in the gym. Training prepares them for game time.

But spiritually speaking, most of us spend very little time training. We spend 99 percent of our time living and less than 1 percent of our time training. We call it "devotions," but we aren't very devoted. We call it "quiet time," but then rush through to tackle the noise of the day. We lack the competitive mind-set that we are facing an opponent. Why don't we approach our spiritual life as a training program? Instead, we often treat it casually. If we're honest, most of us don't even have a plan. And our hit-and-miss approach is littered with excuses: we're too tired or too busy. As a result, we're often spiritually unprepared for the challenges of life.

Bottom line: we want the results without the work. We want to have strong character and faith. We want to be able to weather the storms of life, resist temptation, and walk away from sin. We want to be unselfish, loving, and slow to anger. We want a lot of things, but are we willing to pay the price?

Our *desire* needs to be matched by our *do*. In 1 Timothy 4:7–8, Paul tells us to "train yourselves to be godly. For physical training is of some value, but godliness has value for all things, holding promise for both the present life and the life to come." In 1 Corinthians 9:24–27 we're told to be like athletes training to win the prize. And Ephesians 6:10–18 challenges us to be soldiers ready for battle.

We need a training plan—but we also need to show up and put in some time. We can't be a weekend warrior. There are three Training Truths you must believe for your training to be useful:

1. Training is *always opposed.* Pursuing a relationship with Christ goes against our flesh, the Enemy, the culture, and our schedule. The Enemy does not want us connecting with God and growing in wisdom, so he'll attempt to distract us, discourage us, and overwhelm us with busyness. We'll be tempted to sleep a little longer and skip our training time with God.
2. Training is *often painful* but *always purposeful.* In order to grow, we will need to push and even get a little sore. That's a good thing, even though it may not feel so good at the time. Spiritual muscle grows when it's pushed beyond its limits. And that pain is always a precursor to growth.
3. Training is a *useful means* but a *destructive end.* Training is a means to an end, but it's never meant to be an end in and of itself. Our goal is to be changed into the likeness of Christ. To have the fruit of the spirit growing inside us (Galatians 5:22–25) then showing up on the outside.

If training is your "end," it will become nothing more than religious activity that you check off your list.

If anybody should get this principle, it's athletes and coaches. We know the hours it takes in the gym and on the practice field to produce peak performance. If you want to experience real life-change, you have to train your spirit the same way. So make a sacrifice, get a plan, and show up for the workout. Your soul will get bigger, faster, and stronger, and you'll be ready for the challenges of life. There are no shortcuts to greatness or godliness. We must do the training and let God do the changing.

Be a GameChanger!

Live Intentionally. Maximize Relationships. Pass the Torch.

Live It

What one thing could you do for maximum spiritual growth and life change?

What are some things you could do on a daily basis to increase your spiritual capacity and make your soul bigger, faster, and stronger? How might this impact you in competition?

Read 2 Peter 1:3–4. What has God given you for the journey?

Maximize It

Read Hebrews 12:10–12. Why is the discipline of training often painful? What does this passage say will be the result if we let God change us?

Read Philippians 2:12–14. What does this passage suggest about our role and God's role in the training and changing process?

Read Philippians 4:8 and 2 Timothy 3:16–17. What do these passages suggest about the importance of reading the Word and meditating on it?

Pass It

Grab a teammate and discuss the *WisdomWalks* principle: *We do the training; God does the changing.* What would a spiritual training program look like? Help each other map out and execute a plan. Find ways to encourage coaches and teammates to put in the time and effort to get stronger spiritually. Write down your personal plan below.

My GamePlan

_____

_____

_____

_____

_____

_____

_____

_____

Father, give me the desire and discipline to begin and stick with a spiritual training program that increases the capacity of my heart and soul. Make me bigger, faster, and stronger in character, love, and joy. I know that when I show up and train, You will change me from the inside out and make me a game changer on my team, in my family, and in my community. Amen.

3

COMPETITIVE GREATNESS

WisdomWalks Principle
Be the best you.

*Peace of mind…is a direct result of self-satisfaction in knowing
you made the effort to become the best that you are capable of becoming.*

JOHN WOODEN

Five-time All-Pro Green Bay Packers lineman Jerry Kramer played from 1958 to 1968. Coach Vince Lombardi rode him hard—really hard—in the 1959 preseason. Jerry wanted to quit until one day Coach came through the locker room and told Jerry that he could become the greatest lineman in the NFL. That one encounter with Coach Lombardi transformed Jerry. That day, he decided to give 100 percent to every play in practice and games. And he became one of the greatest linemen, because he understood the concept of competitive greatness! When Lombardi saw more in him and challenged him to use all of his ability, there was a total release of all of his talents, skills, and gifts whenever he competed.

Legendary basketball coach John Wooden coined the phrase "Competitive Greatness." But, as a competitive athlete, I sometimes get it mixed up with "Being Great." Not good! Being the best is striving to be number one. Competitive greatness is not being the best, but being the best you can be. There can only be one best, but everyone can achieve being the best they can be. And there is only one player who can be the best on a team, but a whole team can achieve competitive greatness.

Competitive greatness is learning to rise to every occasion and to push yourself mentally, physically, emotionally, and spiritually to reach your God-given potential. Paul wrote this about competition: "Don't you realize that in a race everyone runs, but only one person gets the prize? So run to win! All athletes are disciplined in their training. They do it to win a prize that will fade away, but we do it for an eternal prize. So I run with purpose in every step" (1 Corinthians 9:24–26 NLT).

Coach Wooden defines competitive greatness as a real love for the hard battle, knowing it offers the opportunity to be at your best when your best is required. These three "Be" principles have helped me grasp competitive greatness:

Be Prepared! It's not about winning, it's about being prepared. Wooden, who would spend thirty minutes teaching his UCLA basketball players how to properly put on socks, said, "I derived great satisfaction from identifying and perfecting those 'trivial' and often troublesome details, because I knew, without doubt, that each one brought UCLA a bit closer to our goal: competitive greatness. If you collect enough pennies, you'll eventually be rich. Each relevant and perfected detail was another penny in our bank." Being prepared is being ready when God opens doors. *There are three O's in life: Opportunities, Obedience, and Outcomes.* It is two parts God and one part you. God creates all opportunities, and He determines the outcomes. Your part is obedience, because you should always be prepared to respond to the Lord's leading. As the classic hymn says, "Trust and obey, for there's no other way." Having a passion to prepare will help you face the battle as an athlete so that challenges are embraced…never feared.

Be Disciplined! If integrity is doing the right thing when no one is watching, then competitive greatness is working hard when no one is watching. *Competitive greatness is a disciplined life.* It is living in such a powerful way that Christ Himself is revealed. God loves good, hard, clean competition. Disciplined athletes have great awareness of the abilities God has blessed them with, and they use those gifts to their full potential to please Jesus. They understand there is a merging of self-discipline and God-provision.

Be Focused! Competitive greatness focuses on a clear vision; it is not sidetracked or distracted. At the 2004 Olympics in Greece, Matt Emmons lost his focus during his last shot of the competition, and it cost him a gold medal in the 50-meter three-position rifle final. While in lane two, he shot at the lane three target. Wrong target. Wrong lane. He had the gold medal won, but he was given a score of zero, dropping him to eighth place. Focus produces a clear picture of the future, and that produces a passion. When athletes have vision burning in their eyes, they become an unstoppable force for the Lord's work. That is playing in the zone! Nobody or nothing can steal the passion that God has placed in your heart as an athlete. By narrowing the focus, the Lord's plan becomes clear because you know the target. When you are focused, you are not sucked into the comparison game and comparing yourself to other teammates. Focus allows you to be the best you by fixing your eyes on the right target—Jesus Christ.

All you have is you. Nothing more; nothing less. Take what God has generously given you and be the best you by unleashing those gifts and talents right where God has placed you. Do it right now...and watch Him do an amazing work through you!

Be a GameChanger!

Live Intentionally. Maximize Relationships. Pass the Torch.

Live It

Name one person in your life who has competitive greatness. Why did you pick that person?

Do you have competitive greatness as an athlete? Why or why not?

Read Hebrews 12:2; 2 Timothy 2:5, 14–16. What do these verses say about being the best God has created you to be? How can you follow through on this wisdom? In what way(s) can you release all your abilities and talents as you compete for Him?

Maximize It

Which biblical character, to you, best defines competitive greatness? Explain.

How can your team have competitive greatness? How about in your relationships?

Reread 1 Corinthians 9:24–27. How can you be prepared as an athlete? Disciplined? Focused?

Pass It

Grab a teammate and discuss the *WisdomWalks* principle: *Be the best you.* How can this simple principle transform your team? Why is it a concept that athletes have such a hard time understanding? How can you help your team be prepared, disciplined, and focused?

My GamePlan

_____

_____

_____

_____

_____

_____

_____

_____

_____

_____

Father, I recognize that You are the Great One. Help me be the best athlete that I can, so people will know You are great—not me. Teach me to play and live in such a way that my life has the power to reveal You. I pray that my play, words, and actions will make You known. I ask for Your assistance so I am prepared, disciplined, and focused. In Jesus' name, amen.

4

PELOTON POWER

WisdomWalks Principle
We're better together.

Sticks in a bundle are unbreakable.
KENYAN PROVERB

For the past seven years, my three sons and I have really gotten into the sport of cycling. Our passion for the sport was fueled by riding together with a handful of friends and watching Lance Armstrong dominate the Tour de France. The Tour is considered the "Super Bowl" of cycling and is arguably one of the most physically, mentally, and spiritually demanding events in all of sports.

For twenty-one stages in just twenty-three days, 180 of the most highly conditioned athletes ride 2,200 miles through some of the most beautiful countryside and grueling mountains in the world. In America, it would be like riding from New York to Las Vegas—on your bike!

You have to work together to win. Winning the Tour without the sacrifice and cooperation of your teammates is impossible. The leader needs every teammate to play their unique role; he depends on the strengths of each. Everybody takes their turn at the front. Some riders bring food and water to the leaders. Others set the pace out front to try to break their opponents. And the coaches and support team in the cars that follow behind shout encouragement and strategy over the radio and rush to repair or replace bikes that break.

Conserving energy by sticking together is the only way for a racer to survive the metabolic equivalent of running twenty-one marathons in twenty-three days. In most stages, a small handful of riders will break away early in the day, creating a lead of ten minutes or more ahead of the pack. That's why the rest of the riders form a large group called a peloton.

Peloton power is similar to what geese experience when they fly in formation, allowing them to fly much farther than they could alone. By flying in a V formation, the flock nearly doubles the distance that one bird could fly on its own. When one goose falls out of formation, it immediately struggles and feels the increased wind resistance, and then "rallies" to get back behind the bird in front. The geese in the back honk encouragement to those up front. Those leading are working hard and need all the encouragement they can get! And, if a goose falls behind, two more geese will drop back to bring the flock back to formation.

For cyclists, teams often ride in a straight line and adjust based on the direction of the wind. Each rider takes his turn leading. But the real power is in the peloton—that large mass of riders working together to conserve energy. With the large group, the reduction in wind resistance is dramatic. In the middle of a large group, riders can literally save up to 40 percent of their energy. And the riders in the peloton almost always catch the breakaway group. If any teammate falls off the back of the peloton, it is very common to see a rider or two go back and work to help them rejoin the group. And at the end of the stage, the riders have far more energy for the next day. Sounds like a great way to compete and to live!

We are better together. We are designed to work together as a team, to bear one another's burdens, and to push each other to do great things. When we are united by the love of Jesus and our mission to share His truth with others, we accomplish much more than we could on our own. In Philippians 1:27 (NLT, 2007), Paul encourages us to stand together in unity.

> *Whether I come and see you again or only hear about you, I will know that you are standing together with one spirit and one purpose, fighting together for the faith, which is the Good News.*

Paul knew that if we don't work toward the same goal, we will fail. But he also knew that each one of us has to play our role. In 1 Corinthians 12:12, 18–19, he paints the picture of teamwork:

> *The body is a unit, though it is made up of many parts; and though all its parts are many, they form one body…in fact God has arranged the parts in the body, every one of them, just as he wanted them to be. If they were all one part, where would the body be?*

That's a great picture of why we need each other as believers in Jesus. We're all part of the same team yet have different roles. Each of us brings unique gifts and talents. Sometimes we get jealous when someone else is in the spotlight, especially if we did a lot of the work behind the scenes. But being a good teammate requires humility. God wants us each to play our specific role and use our unique gifts today to bless others. Your role is just what your teammates need.

Sometimes we're tempted to break away and do life on our own, but it's a lot more work, and in the end, we almost never win. Independence hurts you and the team.

Maybe you are the encourager or the one who pushes your teammates to get better. Maybe your role is to serve. Whatever your role is, know that when you do it well for the sake of the team, we all win. We're better together.

Be a GameChanger!

Live Intentionally. Maximize Relationships. Pass the Torch.

Live It

Have you ever been tempted to break away and do life on your own? What was the result?

What unique gifts and talents do you have that could help your teammates?

Maximize It

Read Romans 15:5–6. How does team unity affect team performance? What happens when one teammate decides it's all about them—their stats, their recognition?

Read Romans 12:3–8. What does it mean that each of us "belongs" to the others?

Why is humility so important in maintaining the cohesiveness of the team?

Pass It

Grab a teammate and discuss the *WisdomWalks* principle: *We're better together.* How can each of you play a role in building team unity? What is currently dividing your team and hurting your performance? Find ways to encourage coaches and teammates to put in the time and effort to discover their spiritual role on the team.

My GamePlan

_____

_____

_____

_____

_____

_____

_____

_____

Father, thank You for designing each of us with unique gifts and talents to bring to Your team. Help me discover the role You want me to play to build team unity on the field and off. Help me to do whatever I can to make my teammates better. Help me to set aside my own desires for the good of the team. I know that we are better together. Amen.

5

REAL DEAL

WisdomWalks Principle
You can't fake the Almighty.

When wealth is lost, nothing is lost; when health is lost,
something is lost; when character is lost, all is lost.
BILLY GRAHAM

Every day it sits on my desk as a powerful reminder. It tugs on my soul with a convicting message: "Be careful. Do not let your life be like this." The object is a gorgeous leather Bible with all the extras, including gold-tipped pages. It looks really nice on the outside, but when you crack open the pages, they're blank. Yup—not a single word or letter. It appears to be the Bible of all Bibles on the outside but contains nothing of God's message on the inside.

This fake Bible was actually a sample sent to me by a publisher so we could get an idea of a cover we wanted for a future FCA Bible. But it motivates me every day to be the real deal—to be authentic and make sure nothing gets in the way of my following Christ. Truthfully, there are gaps in all of us. We're more like that Bible than we might think! On the surface, we may look a certain way, but in our hearts we may feel totally different.

This dichotomy easily leaks into the world of sports. As competitors, we're constantly pushed to perform and to look good. We value the external over the internal, the public over the private. And we learn to cover up our "stuff" and fake it. We want others to think we are better athletes than we are. We get pulled into the trap of posing—looking good and impressing others. *We become experts at covering up our true selves because we think people won't like who we really are.* We actually believe the fake version of us is what people want, and that faking it covers the hurts, fears, wounds, and gaps, and tucks all that bad stuff conveniently away. But Proverbs 28:13–14 (NIV, 2011) warns us about what happens when we fake it and bury our junk: "Whoever conceals their sins does not prosper, but the one who confesses and renounces them finds mercy. Blessed is the one who always trembles before God, but whoever hardens their heart falls into trouble."

God has a way of slicing through all of that. His touch grips our souls and exposes our faking. It can be risky to be real, but *you can't play it safe when it comes to following Christ.* Nowhere in Scripture does Jesus encourage us to surrender our lives to Him so that life will get easier. The Lord's call always touches the very thing we don't want to give up.

Mark 10:21–22 (MSG) records a conversation Jesus had with a successful businessman:

> *Jesus looked him hard in the eye—and loved him! He said, "There's one thing left: Go sell whatever you own and give it to the poor. All your wealth will then be heavenly wealth. And come follow me."*
>
> *The man's face clouded over. This was the last thing he expected to hear, and he walked off with a heavy heart. He was holding on tight to a lot of things, and not about to let go.*

Jesus basically said, "Hey, rich man, give up your wealth and follow Me." The rich man went away sad, because Jesus pinpointed the very thing that the man wanted to hold back. The issue wasn't that he was rich, but that his wealth got in the way of his following Christ.

What one thing do you have left? We all have something that gets in the way of our being all-in, of our loving Jesus the way we should. If Jesus said to you, "Hey, athlete/coach, give up your (blank) and follow Me," what would He say?

God wants us to be the real deal. You can't fake it and have integrity at the same time. The Oxford English Dictionary says integrity comes from the Latin word *integritas*, which means "wholeness, entireness, or completeness." The root word is *integer*, which means "untouched, intact, or entire." Warren Wiersbe says:

> *Integrity is to personal or corporate character what health is to the body or 20/20 vision is to the eyes. A person with integrity is not divided (that's duplicity) or merely pretending (that's hypocrisy). He or she is "whole"; life is "put together," and things are working together harmoniously.*

Integrity is basically being solid, rocklike. We read in Proverbs 11:3 the powerful impact of integrity: "The integrity of the upright guides them, but the unfaithful are destroyed by their duplicity."

Integrity is hard for two reasons. First, it takes guts to be transparent and not fake it. When you get real, teammates will be drawn to your authenticity. It always happens. When you become an open book, it doesn't push them away but instead brings them closer. Their respect, trust, and love for you will increase. Second, integrity requires courage to do what is right even when it is hard. Many times you'll be the only one pursuing a life of integrity and authenticity. As a follower of Christ, it might mean standing alone as a result of your convictions, but God will honor it.

So what's holding you back from experiencing Christ's power? Identify that one thing. Bring it into the light, and let God's touch heal it. Just think how different your life would be. No more faking. No more posing. No more covering up. You can't fake your integrity or your faith, because you can never fake the Almighty. Be a competitor full of integrity.

Be a GameChanger!

Live Intentionally. Maximize Relationships. Pass the Torch.

Live It

Read all of the rich man's story in Mark 10:17–22. What did the rich man want? What got in his way? As a competitor, what gets in your way of following Jesus?

Why do we pretend to be one thing on the outside when we're different on the inside? How do you "pose"? How would your teammates answer this question about you?

Read also 2 Corinthians 5:17. What does this verse say about "the old you" and the "new you"? How might the new you look different to your teammates?

Maximize It

Why do you think it's so hard to be authentic? Explain.

Read 1 Chronicles 29:10–20. What kinds of things did David thank the Lord for? What does verse 17 say about how the Lord responds to integrity?

As an athlete, when has your integrity been tested? What happened as a result?

Pass It

Grab a teammate and discuss the *WisdomWalks* principle: *You can't fake the Almighty.* Be honest with your teammate. Have you ever "faked it"? How does faking it impact your team? How can being the real deal impact the culture of your entire team?

My GamePlan

_____

_____

_____

_____

_____

_____

Father, thank You for Your faithfulness in helping me change. It has become too natural for me to live a fake life. I want to be the real deal. I want to be an athlete of integrity. Show me the gaps. Forgive me for letting anything get between You and me. I ask for Your touch today. In Jesus' name, I pray, amen.

6

ROOKIE RUSH

WisdomWalks Principle
Think like a rookie; play like a pro.

*Rookies put their head down, work hard, stay positive, live fearlessly,
and are naïve enough to be successful.
Let the rookie mind-set fuel your optimism and passion.*

JON GORDON

One of my favorite sports movies is *The Rookie*. It's the story of Jimmy Morris, a pitcher who had his single-A minor-league baseball career cut short by injuries and saw his dream of playing in the big leagues disappear. Years later, when he was a high school baseball coach, his players challenged him to start to "bring the heat" in batting practice so they could get better. When he did, their jaws dropped; he was throwing with unhittable velocity. The boys then challenged him again—this time saying that if they won the district championship (something they had never done), he would get a tryout with the majors and could give it one last shot.

The team won the title, and Jimmy got his shot. He became, at the age of thirty-five, the "Oldest Rookie" to pitch in the majors. His trip to the big leagues was marked by the *rookie rush*—the things that all rookies feel and experience when they get their shot. I felt the rookie rush in high school when I was called up to the varsity for baseball and basketball as an underclassman. I'll never forget that adrenaline rush that causes butterflies in your stomach. The Rookie Rush has five key characteristics that provide fuel for everything we do: Passion, Belief, Humility, Gratitude, and Intensity.

Rookies have *passion*. They are fueled by their love of the game. I still remember the excitement of putting on the uniform and hitting the field. Rookies live, eat, and breathe their sport, and their passion breeds a single-minded focus that makes them great. But that same passion and undivided focus for your sport is meant to take a backseat to your love and passion for Christ: "Love the Lord your God with all your heart and with all your soul and with all your mind and with all your strength" (Mark 12:30).

Passion and purpose get us out of bed in the morning. Knowing we are pursuing God and His greatness fuels our focus and drives us to greatness.

Rookies have *belief*. They believe in the impossible. They have an unquenchable optimism and expect great things to happen. They don't know what can't be done. They don't have limits. Jesus said: "What is impossible with men is possible with God (Luke 18:27).

This optimistic, will-not-be-denied belief is what champions are made of. When facing Goliath, David believed in God's power over his problem. He was willing to take a risk that no one else would take. He was the "rookie," and he believed God. The "veterans" laughed—and some probably thought he was crazy. But with God's victory through David, all the veterans came back to life (and faith). Every single victory in Scripture and in life is preceded by belief. Belief forms the foundation of all life and faith!

Rookies have *humility*. They know they have a lot to learn from the veterans and they have to earn the respect of their teammates. They are willing to serve, to carry the bags, to pick up after practice, to go the extra mile to serve their coaches and teammates.

When we model humility, God sees it. He loves it. And He rewards it. "Do nothing out of selfish ambition or vain conceit, *but in humility consider others better than yourselves. Each of you should look not only to your own interests, but also to the interests of others*" (Philippians 2:3–4 emphasis added.

Sometimes rookies think it shows a lack of confidence to be humble, but it actually demonstrates extreme internal strength. And it builds relational trust that can't be earned any other way.

Rookies have *gratitude*. They recognize the opportunity they've been given and take nothing for granted. They have a mix of confidence and dependence, giving thanks for everything, even the little things. And yes, even for the challenges. "So then, just as you received Christ Jesus as Lord, continue to live in him, rooted and built up in him, strengthened in the faith as you were taught, *and overflowing with thankfulness*" (Colossians 2:6–7 emphasis added)

Our attitude of gratitude must overflow. So thank the team managers, thank the trainers, thank the referees and the coaches, and thank your teammates. Gratitude is contagious.

Rookies have *intensity*. They are willing to do whatever it takes to make it. They go above and beyond. They get to practice early. They stay late for additional work. All of Jesus' disciples knew intensity—how to pursue the prize and how to combat the Enemy with diligence. "But one thing I do: Forgetting what is behind and *straining toward what is ahead*, I press on toward the goal to win the prize for which God has called me heavenward in Christ Jesus" (Philippians 3:13–14 emphasis added).

Rookies make mistakes, no doubt about it. And veterans have a lot of wisdom and experience to pass on to the new kids on the block! But veterans can learn a lot from rookies. They have the spirit to take instruction and learn along the way. They are hungry and humble. And they never feel entitled to anything or expect special treatment. If we are continuously fueled by the rookie rush—passion, belief, humility, gratitude, and intensity—we'll become the best we can be. And we'll make everybody else better along the way.

Be a GameChanger!

Live Intentionally. Maximize Relationships. Pass the Torch.

Live It

Do you have the Rookie Rush? Or have you lost some of the passion and intensity for the game? Explain.

Of the five key characteristics of a rookie, which do you struggle with most? What do you have in abundance?

Maximize It

Read Mark 9:17–24. What does this story tell us about the power of belief in Jesus? When doubt creeps in, how can the prayer in verse 24 change our perspective?

What can you do to create the rookie rush with your team? In what specific ways can you merge the experience and wisdom of the veterans with the Rookie Rush?

Pass It

Grab a teammate and discuss the *WisdomWalks* principle: *Think like a rookie; play like a pro.* How can you help to reestablish passion, belief, and intensity mixed with humility and gratitude in the entire team?

My GamePlan

_____

_____

_____

_____

_____

_____

_____

_____

_____

Father, thank You for the opportunity to play and compete. Reignite in me a spirit of passion, belief, and intensity for living and growing in Christ. Let me not take anything for granted, knowing that life is a gift. Help me to live with a spirit of humility, believing that nothing is impossible for those who believe. And give me an attitude of gratitude always. Amen.

7

THE PACER

WisdomWalks Principle
Run with Jesus.

Enoch walked with God.
Genesis 5:24

After putting on my GPS running watch, I was all set for the Kansas City Half-Marathon. As I got out of my car and headed toward the starting line, I was looking forward to joining the other eleven thousand runners on a beautiful, crisp fall morning. Turning on my watch that I'd charged the night before, I was shocked it didn't show any signs of life. It had been on all night, and the battery was dead! My goal to beat my personal record in the half-marathon with a 1:25 seemed out of the question. How would I maintain my pace without my watch? Every marathon I've run, I've always had my watch. I didn't know what to do. A runner without a watch is like a fish out of water.

Approaching the starting line, I saw several runners with bright green shirts holding signs with numbers on them. That's when I remembered the marathon pacer group leaders! *Pacers are runners who help the runners achieve their goal times.* Never having run with a pacer before, I decided this was my only chance to reach my goal. I finally found my pacer, Zach, who was carrying the 1:25 sign. Ten of us gathered around Zach with the goal to finish with him. There was no pressure to remain with the group, but Zach would keep us on track. No stops, no breaks, no waiting for stragglers. He set the pace, and it was our job to stay with him.

The entire race, I stayed on Zach's hip, stride for stride. I didn't worry about my time, my pace, or my splits. Zach took care of everything. He not only tracked the time, but he encouraged us, motivated us, and gave us tips throughout the run. All I needed to do was run with Zach, step by step. When eight runners fell back, Zach didn't slow. He maintained the pace needed to accomplish the goal on his sign. Only two of us crossed the finish line with Zach. As we crossed the finish line, I was amazed by the simplicity of the race. I never looked at my watch. I just ran with Zach. It was freeing!

As athletes and coaches, we often make sports too complicated. We think we need all the right equipment, clothing, advice, and training. Even though there is a place for all those things, the "stuff" becomes more important than the goal, making sports complicated instead of simple… overwhelming instead of freeing.

Relying on all the "stuff" also becomes a part of the way we approach God. Instead of getting into stride with Jesus, we pick up the new book, download a podcast, or ask others for their thoughts. Oswald Chambers gets it right when he writes, *"Getting into the stride of God means nothing less than union with Himself."*

Let's cut through all the fluff and stuff. The goal is union with Jesus Christ. We need to get into the stride of God by being in step with Him. When we decide to walk with God, we have to know His pace, know His ways. And when we get into His stride, the only thing that matters is the life of Christ.

Enoch and Noah are two great examples of WisdomWalkers who knew what it meant to have God as their Pacer. Genesis 5:24 (HCSB) says, "Enoch walked with God." Genesis 6:9 (HCSB) says, "Noah was a righteous man, blameless among his contemporaries; Noah walked with God." When we walk with God, we will impact lives not only in our generation but in the generations to come! Enoch was Noah's great-grandfather. Because of Enoch's example, generation after generation learned to walk with God.

Oswald Chambers continues his thoughts on striding when he writes, "It takes a long time to get there, but keep at it. Don't give in because the pain is bad just now, get on with it, and before long you will find you have a new vision and a new purpose." *As our Pacer, Jesus desires for us to simply run with Him.* He's holding a sign that says, "Love God with all you have!" In Matthew 22:37–38 (HCSB), our Pacer communicates the Greatest Commandment: "Love the Lord your God with all your heart, with all your soul, and with all your mind. This is the greatest and most important command."

If you need to get your second wind spiritually, it's time to take your first step. In Colossians 2:6–7 (MSG), Paul encourages us to "get off go" and start running with Jesus:

My counsel for you is simple and straightforward: Just go ahead with what you've been given. You received Christ Jesus, the Master; now live *him. You're deeply rooted in him. You're well constructed upon him. You know your way around the faith. Now do what you've been taught. School's out; quit studying the subject and start* living *it! And let your living spill over into thanksgiving.*

Take one step with Him. This one step of faith with Jesus can develop into a daily walk. As our Pacer, all He asks us is that we take one step at a time with Him, side by side. Get in stride with the Pacer and run with Jesus!

Be a GameChanger!

Live Intentionally. Maximize Relationships. Pass the Torch.

Live It

When you evaluate the world of sports, how do you think athletes and coaches get caught up with the fluff and stuff?

Read Psalm 119:1–3; 2 Corinthians 5:7; Hebrews 11:5. What do these verses say about keeping in stride with the Pacer and living by faith?

Is it easy or hard for you personally to think of Jesus as your Pacer? If it's hard, what holds you back from running side by side with Jesus?

Maximize It

What does it mean to "walk with God"? In what ways did Enoch and Noah walk with God?

Read Hebrews 12:1–2. What sins easily entangle athletes and weigh them down? Why do you think this is? What's the solution?

How can you be freed up to run with Jesus? What first step could you take this week to get in stride with your Pacer?

Pass It

Grab a teammate and discuss the *WisdomWalks* principle: *Run with Jesus.* What could the two of you do to walk more closely with Jesus? Imagine what could happen if you could get at least 10 percent of your team walking with Jesus. Brainstorm specific ways you could impact your whole team.

My GamePlan

_____

_____

_____

_____

_____

_____

_____

Lord, my goal is to love You with everything I have. As my Pacer, help me to run the race of faith You've marked before me. I ask for the perseverance and endurance that are needed so that I remain focused on You, instead of the stuff that weighs me down. Thank You for Your love and grace when I need it. In the name of Jesus, I pray, amen.

8

THE GAME PLAN

WisdomWalks Principle
If you want to win, follow the Plan.

He who fails to plan plans to fail.
SIR WINSTON CHURCHILL

Have you ever seen a coach in the NFL calling plays on the sideline from that color-coded, laminated "game plan"? I've always wanted to see one of those up close and personal. And recently, a close friend of mine who has been coaching in the NFL for well over a decade gave me a rare glimpse—an insider's look, if you will—at a typical offensive game plan. In fact, the plan he showed me was the one his team had used to drub my favorite team just two weeks earlier!

This offensive game plan was a foreign language to me, but it spelled out the plays that would be called under just about every possible situation—opening drive, short yardage, red zone, goal line, two-minute drill, and no-huddle. It spelled out plays by down and yardage needed. It included passes and runs and even accounted for whether they were ahead or behind on the scoreboard. And the plan was designed to cater to what the team did best and anticipate what the opponent would do.

All coaches put together a game plan that they believe puts them in the best position to win. They may study the film of the opponent to figure out their "schemes," and they coach their own players to make sure they properly execute all the plays that are called. There is an offensive game plan designed to put points on the board and a defensive game plan designed to stop the opposition.

God has given us a "game plan" for life. It's called the Bible. Many people think that it's just a rule book, telling us right and wrong with a bunch of "do's and don'ts." But it's really more a book about how to live.

All Scripture is inspired by God and is useful to teach us what is true and to make us realize what is wrong in our lives. It corrects us when we are wrong and teaches us to do what is right. God uses it to prepare and equip his people to do every good work.

2 Timothy 3:16–17 nlt

In life, we need an offensive and defensive game plan as well. The Word gives us plenty of instruction for how to put points on the board. It teaches us how to love, serve, encourage, and forgive. It teaches us how to be generous with our money, our time, and even our words. It tells us how to speak words of life, build relationships based on trust, handle conflict, handle our money, and even how to get back on track if we've failed. We are taught how to share our faith, pray, and engage in the supernatural battle. The Word brings a change of heart and a change of behavior.

It also tells us how to shut down our opponent. It teaches us how to flee from temptation, get out of compromising situations, stand up for what's right, and stand against what's wrong. The Word gives us wisdom for combating the attempts of the Enemy to discourage, defeat, divide, and destroy us. It shows us how to reconcile damaged relationships, how to overcome fear with faith, and how to combat our old nature with its desires, pride, and selfishness. And above all else, we learn how to guard our hearts.

God uses His Word to get us ready for competition—to equip us for every play and every day. The Word of God contains wisdom necessary for living a life worthy of the Lord. And it has the power to expose our attitudes and even the motives of our hearts.

For the word of God is living and active. Sharper than any double-edged sword, it penetrates even to dividing soul and spirit, joints and marrow; it judges the thoughts and attitudes of the heart.

Hebrews 4:12

It acts as a supernatural mirror that allows us to see inside and get to the heart of our issues. And it's a lamp to our feet and a light for our path.

We have to study the game plan in order to be ready for the game and our opponent. It would be absurd to suggest that the coach put a plan together, only to have the athletes ignore it and abandon it once the game starts. What would be the point?

God has assembled His game plan for life. He wants us to know it inside and out and follow it. He's given us plays to run no matter what situation we face. He has all the answers. All we have to do is execute the plan.

But in order to know the plays, we first have to study the plan. Only then can we defeat our opponent. So why not spend some time in the Word today? If you want to win, follow the plan.

Be a GameChanger!

Live Intentionally. Maximize Relationships. Pass the Torch.

Live It

If you think of God's Word as your game plan for a victorious life, packed with all the wisdom you need for every situation, how does that change your perspective of its importance?

If you were to try to execute this plan, are you prepared? Have you studied it? Why or why not? How might its wisdom help you in a current life situation?

If you prepared for your sport the way you prepare for life, how would you do in competition?

Maximize It

Read 2 Peter 1:3. What does it mean that we have been given everything we need for life and godliness? What have we been given?

Read Psalm 33:11; Proverbs 16:9; Jeremiah 29:11. What do these passages indicate about God's plans for us? About our own plans? Why is following God's plan a guaranteed win?

Pass It

Grab a teammate and discuss the *WisdomWalks* principle—*If you want to win, follow the plan.* How much time, on average, do each of you spend studying God's Word each day or week? Will that kind of investment get you fit and ready for the battles of life? Why or why not? Commit to specific goals to get in the Word daily.

My GamePlan

_____

_____

_____

_____

_____

_____

_____

_____

_____

Father, I believe that Your Word—the Bible—is my Game Plan for life. I believe every word was inspired by You for my benefit, training, and instruction. I also believe that Your plan has answers for all my questions and gives wisdom and direction for my everyday issues. Help me to be diligent to study the Plan and execute it each day. Amen.

9

GOOD FOR NOTHING

WisdomWalks Principle
Don't worry; be praying.

*Worrying doesn't empty tomorrow of its sorrow,
it empties today of its strength.*
Corrie ten Boom

My freshman year at college, I was so stressed out I was ready to explode. Seventy-five players were competing for thirty-five spots for the University of Delaware lacrosse team. If that wasn't tough enough, almost the entire team had returned with only a few spots to fill. Even though the coach had recruited me, the team's Top 10 national ranking the year before had brought him a great recruiting class.

I phoned my mom. "I don't think I'm going to make the team," I told her. I worried that my dream of playing college lacrosse was dying, so I did what I do really well: I began to question everything. *Why did I come to Delaware? What will people think if I get cut? Should I transfer if I don't make the team?* Worry consumed me.

Worry has no redeeming value. It's *good for nothing*—a descriptive phrase that connotes uselessness or lack of value in people, objects, or things. (In fact, I can think of a lot of good-for-nothing objects in my garage and basement collecting dust.) To say the least, good for nothing isn't a positive, encouraging phrase. I've never heard anyone say, "Thanks for calling me a good-for-nothing!"

In Philippians 4:6 (REB), the apostle Paul says, "In nothing be anxious; but in everything by prayer and supplication with thanksgiving let your requests be made known unto God."

Sometimes we believe worry will actually help and protect us from danger. But justifying an unhealthy emotion is unwise. Worry is plain wrong. It rots and destroys the mind. It drains us and ties us down. It becomes cancer on a team. As Proverbs 12:25 (NLT) says, "Worry weighs us down."

The actual word *worry* is derived from the German word *wurgen*, which means "to strangle, to choke." Worry strangles our hearts and minds with the world's viewpoint and chokes out God's viewpoint.

Worry always asks the question "What if?" This question plagues athletes, keeping them from living with purpose and meaning. *What if I don't make the team? What if I get hurt? What if the coach doesn't like me? What if the other players don't accept me? What if I lose my starting position?* Worry…worry…worry.

The good news is that we cannot control the future. If we knew with certainty what the future holds for us, then we wouldn't need to trust God.

Great Certainty = Little Trust.
Little Certainty = Great Trust.
Great Control = Little Trust.
Little Control = Great Trust.

The problem is, we want to have it both ways: we want great certainty, great control, and also great trust. *Lord, I want to know for sure what is going to happen, and then I will have great trust and won't worry.* Instead, we should pray: "Lord, I have no idea what the future may bring, but regardless, I will have unwavering trust and will not worry." Oswald Chambers says, "The one great crime on the part of the disciple, according to Jesus Christ, is worry. Whenever we begin to calculate without God, we commit sin."

How should we respond to worry? Jesus shoots it to us straight in Matthew 6:31–34:

Do not worry, saying, "What shall we eat?" or "What shall we drink?" or "What shall we wear?"… But seek first his kingdom and his righteousness, and all these things will be given to you as well. Therefore do not worry about tomorrow, for tomorrow will worry about itself. Each day has enough trouble of its own.

Worry is the absolute faith that God will screw up. Where there is worry and anxiety, we have fear and lack of trust. When you have faith and trust, you have peace and joy.

Praying for everything is the antidote. Bobby McFerrin's song "Don't Worry, Be Happy" is a tune that can get stuck in our minds. You are probably singing it now just from seeing the words! However, we should change it to "Don't Worry, Be Praying." Max Lucado said, "No one can pray and worry at the same time." As a WisdomWalker, our lives should be rooted in prayer. Prayer conquers worry and increases trust. Prayer reminds us that we cannot control the future, but we will trust the One who can.

My mom's a wise woman. When I made that worried phone call, she asked, "If God solved your problem, what would you like the answer to be?"

"Make the team," I said.

"Well, then, pray to that end. *Prayer and trust go hand in hand.*"

I was convicted. I had done a ton of worrying, but not much praying. I decided to change that. Over the next several weeks, my faith and prayer drove out my worry and anxiety. Making the team wasn't even the miracle—better yet, God cultivated a rich prayer life in me that's strong to this day.

Competitors, refuse to worry. Instead, trust God and pray about every part of your life—sports, family, friends, school, and church. Don't worry; be praying!

Be a GameChanger!

Live Intentionally. Maximize Relationships. Pass the Torch.

Live It

Do you consider yourself a worrier? Why or why not?

As an athlete, what do you worry about the most? What "what if" questions do you ask?

Read Psalm 37:25; Matthew 6:33; Luke 12:29. What do these verses say about worry—and faith? In what specific ways could you increase your faith?

Maximize It

Who—a teammate, friend, mentor—could help you control the worry habit? And how? What step can you take today on the journey toward becoming worry free?

What areas of life do you need to release to God to break the worry habit? How can you increase your trust in God?

Read James 4:13–14. How does worry drain our time and strength? If a culture of worry can destroy a team, then what kind of culture can build a team?

Pass It

Grab a teammate and discuss the *WisdomWalks* principle: *Don't worry; be praying.* How can this principle impact your team? Brainstorm specific ways to drive out worry among the players and coaches.

My GamePlan

_____

_____

_____

_____

_____

_____

Lord God in heaven, I know worry is sin. It truly is good for nothing. Forgive me for worrying and renew my mind today. Drain the worry out of my heart. When I compete for You, remind me of a simple truth: that You are in control and I am not. In the name of Jesus, I pray, amen.

10

BETTER—OR DEADER?

WisdomWalks Principle
You need to die to live.

The more a man dies to himself, the more he begins to live unto God.
THOMAS À KEMPIS

Coach Sleepy Thompson coached football at my high school for thirty-two years. His teams boasted twenty-nine winning seasons, twelve conference titles, and three undefeated seasons. It was an honor and blessing to be a member of one of those undefeated seasons. Coach Thompson had a gift for taking whatever boys came through the door (including myself) and turning them into winners. I loved playing for Coach Thompson. As a true competitor, I always had an internal drive to become a better football player, but he coached in such a way that the entire team was taken to a higher level of competition.

Personally, I'm fascinated with what makes a great coach like Sleepy Thompson. The word *coach* actually comes from the word *stagecoach*, implying that they take passengers from point A to point B. Coach Thompson knew where he wanted his teams to go, even though players like me didn't have a clue. His point B was very well defined, with a clear destination.

In life, our Master Coach, Jesus Christ, also has a clear game plan for us. He wants us to get from point A to point B, but sometimes I think we get His point B mixed up with our own assumptions about what the Christian life should be. We think God wants us to get better—to improve, become better people, or to be nicer Christians. But His call goes much deeper than that. Just look at how He challenged His followers and the leaders of the day. He never encouraged them to get better but, instead, deader. That's right, deader. Romans 6:11 (HCSB) says, "So, you too consider yourselves dead to sin, but alive to God in Christ Jesus."

Since we only die once, how can we get deader? By recognizing our brokenness and sacrificing ourselves daily. In Romans 12:1 (NIV, 2011), Paul urges us to offer our bodies as a living sacrifice:

> *Therefore, I urge you, brothers and sisters, in view of God's mercy, to offer your bodies as a living sacrifice, holy and pleasing to God—this is your true and proper worship.*

The problem with a living sacrifice is that it can crawl off the altar—and we often do! But Jesus always flipped around the conventional wisdom of the day. His teaching and training on what it meant to be an authentic disciple didn't fall in line with the world and its point of view. If you wanted to be rich, He said you should give it all way. If you wanted to be a leader, He taught that you should become a servant. If you wanted to be a friend, He said you should give up your life. If you wanted to live, He said you must die. The apostle Paul wrote in Galatians 2:20, "I have been crucified with Christ." That's what it means to get deader. When Paul wrote this, he didn't mean physical death. He was talking about dying to our desires. Getting deader is dying to yourself daily!

The great German theologian Dietrich Bonhoeffer wrote, "When Christ calls a man, He bids him come and die." It's a radical call that doesn't give us warm, fuzzy feelings. It cuts through the surface, pierces the heart, and grips our soul. We realize we can't play it safe when it comes to following Christ. Nowhere in Scripture does Jesus encourage us to surrender our life to Him and just get better. Instead, His call always touches the very thing we do not want to give up. Paul understood what Jesus was asking His followers to do when he wrote in Galatians 5:24 (ESV), "And those who belong to Christ Jesus have crucified the flesh with its passions and desires."

All of us need to wake up each day and say, "I choose to die today!" What are we doing about it? That's what it means to get deader. We have to identify the passions and desires that get in the way of being all in, examine it, dig it out, and die to it.

Jesus wants us to get to a new place spiritually, but it probably won't be the place we thought we were going. It will be an unexpected point B mapped out by our Master Coach. He has a way of transforming us each day, but only if we are willing to crawl up on the altar and offer ourselves as a living sacrifice.

The sports world is longing to see competitors that are dead to self. But it's all or nothing. You can't do it halfway. Jesus wants us to die to the things of this world—our selfish desires, our comfort. He never said it would be easy. However, to really live, you need to die.

Let's become deader, not just better!

═══════════════╱ **Be a GameChanger!** ╲═══════════════

Live Intentionally. Maximize Relationships. Pass the Torch.

Live It

Have you ever had a coach like Sleepy Thompson? If so, what made that coach great? Did your coach help get the team from point A to point B? Explain that journey.

How does your Master Coach, Jesus Christ, want to coach you up? What game plan do you think He has for you (that might be very different from you own)? Why?

Read Mark 9:35; Luke 17:33; Romans 6:6–12; 2 Corinthians 12:9; 1 Peter 5:6. What one thing needs to die in you? How can these verses encourage you to take the first step in putting that thing on the altar?

Maximize It

Read Romans 12:1–2. How can you be a living sacrifice on your team? What does it mean to sacrifice as a competitor?

How do you respond to Dietrich Bonhoeffer's quote, "When Christ calls a man, He bids him come and die"? What do you think the Lord wants you to do about it? How could you respond daily to this call?

Pass It

Grab a teammate and discuss the *WisdomWalks* principle: *You need to die to live.* How might your dying to self daily impact your teammates? What would it look like for your entire team to follow this *WisdomWalks* principle?

My GamePlan

_____

_____

_____

_____

_____

_____

_____

_____

_____

_____

Father, I want to get deader. I'm not completely sure what that means—or how to do it—but I'm asking You to help me on this journey. There are things in my life that prevent me from being all in…things that hold me back. Reveal to me what it means to be a living sacrifice. Help me die to self daily. I want to get deader, so I can live for You. Amen.

11

MOVE THOSE CHAINS

WisdomWalks Principle
Consistency leads to excellence.

Inconsistency is the only thing in which men are consistent.
HORACE SMITH

My youngest son plays in a flag-football league with a bunch of his friends, and I get to coach. One of the keys to the game is getting a first down by moving the ball across midfield so you can get four more downs to score. And getting first downs is critical at all levels of football.

Every time my family goes to a Baltimore Ravens football game we get caught up in signaling and chanting "Move those chains!" every time the Ravens get a first down. At first glance you might think, *Big deal. They moved the ball ten yards. They didn't put any points on the scoreboard.* But when you realize that every first down gets you closer to your goal, you understand how important it really is. First downs keep the drive alive; they keep our offense on the field with our opponent's defense trying to stop us.

In the NFL, the teams that play with the most consistency—those who have the most time of possession and the fewest turnovers and penalties—win the most games. It's really that simple. This is true in almost every sport. The player or team that *practices, prepares,* and *performs* with the most consistency generally outplays their opponent. And when we "move the chains," we create and sustain momentum.

Consistency leads to continuous, forward progress. It's defined by being steady, reliable, and persistent. Inconsistency, on the other hand, is the enemy of excellence. It takes shortcuts. It makes excuses. And it leads to a breakdown of trust and a lack of progress and improvement. It's one step forward, two steps back.

Consistency is fueled by self-discipline and diligence. Solomon describes how one of God's smallest creations is powerful because of its diligent activity.

Go to the ant, you sluggard; consider its ways and be wise! It has no commander, no overseer or ruler, yet it stores its provisions in summer and gathers its food at harvest.

PROVERBS 6:6–8

Unfortunately, many of us don't see that what we do today affects who we become tomorrow. Many think that they can let loose for a season and that it will have no effect on their character or their health or their future. But let's face it—what we do today is going to affect us down the road. Sometimes the result is immediate, while other times it may take time to surface.

Being consistent is one of the most difficult things to execute. It doesn't come naturally for most people—we have to work at it—especially if we're striving for excellence. When you are consistent, people can count on you; they know what to expect. They see that you are the same person no matter what the circumstance. They know you are willing to do whatever it takes.

Moving the chains simply means that you will do what it takes to reach your goal. It means doing the little things that lead to growth. And it means doing the hard things—even when you want to quit, even when you don't feel like it, even when you're tired, even when you can't see the results, and even when things don't seem to be going the way you think they should.

As competitors, we know how to train consistently in the gym. We know how to spend hour after hour practicing to get better. We know the right foods to eat and how much rest we need. We know how this pays off. If we train in the off-season, go the extra mile in practice, and pay attention to the little things, we get bigger, faster, and stronger. If we take shortcuts and compromise, we'll find out on game day.

But how many of us apply that same diligence in our spiritual life? Do we train ourselves in godliness? Or are we hit-and-miss? Do we spend time digging in His Word? Do we surrender daily to His plans? If we continue to pursue God, spend time seeking Him daily, and follow Him, we will become more and more like Jesus. If we're on-again, off-again, we won't be prepared for the challenges of life. It's that simple.

And without faith it is impossible to please God, because anyone who comes to him must believe that he exists and that he rewards those who earnestly seek him.

HEBREWS 11:6

God rewards us when we seek Him. Are the things that you're doing on a daily basis preparing you for what and who you hope to become in the future?

A consistent life leads to both internal transformation and external influence. So let's strive to take action and do the little things that lead to excellence. Let's move those chains.

Be a GameChanger!

Live Intentionally. Maximize Relationships. Pass the Torch.

Live It

As a coach or competitor preparing for sport, how would you describe your level of consistency—and why?

1. Nonexistent   2. On and off   3. Daily

Read Luke 9:23–24. As a follower of Christ, how would you describe your level of spiritual consistency—and why?

1. Nonexistent   2. On and off   3. Daily

What one thing could you do daily that would lead to the biggest spiritual life-change?

Maximize It

Read Proverbs 2:1–5. What does this passage imply about the effort required to uncover God's wisdom for life?

What are you willing to sacrifice to make time to pursue consistent time with God?

Read Matthew 5:6. How could applying this verse change your consistency in pursuing God?

Pass It

Grab a teammate and discuss the *WisdomWalks* principle: *Consistency leads to excellence.* How could you get consistent spiritual time with those interested on your team? Talk with your teammates and coaches about the possibility of a team Bible study or pre-game prayer.

My GamePlan

_____

_____

_____

_____

_____

_____

_____

_____

_____

_____

Father, I pray that You would give me a powerful desire for consistent time with You. Help me to dig into Your Word daily and to surrender my plans to You. Help me to carve out regular time for study and prayer and help me to be diligent, even when I feel tired or distant. Help me to stop making excuses. Prepare me for the challenges of competition, the classroom, and life by helping me build on the truth of Your Word. Change me from the inside out. Amen.

12

FUN FACTOR

WisdomWalks Principle
If it's fun, it gets done.

When you have fun, it changes all the pressure to pleasure.
KEN GRIFFEY JR.

When I was coaching rec lacrosse for my sons, I loved making practice fun. But the "funnest" thing we ever did was to play pick-up football at the end of practice as a reward! Instead of doing speed and agility work, I took a football out of my lacrosse bag, let them split up the teams, wound 'em up, and let 'em go! You would have thought I'd given the boys a Christmas present! They made up their own plays, some of which were pretty creative, and they ran harder than they ever did in practice. But the overwhelming emotion was pure joy. They laughed and celebrated. They high-fived and danced in the end zone! It was a sight to see. And they even came together more as a team!

At the start of every practice, the boys would run and check my bag. "Are we playing football today?" Other times we played Wiffle Ball with the exact same result. It kept things fresh. The lesson I learned as a coach was this: it's gotta be fun. After all, it's called a *game* for a reason. We play it; we don't "work" it. Games are supposed to be fun, but we often suck the fun out of it. We make it work and then wonder why most of our kids buckle under the pressure and end up quitting by the time they hit middle school.

In every youth sports survey, the number-one reason kids quit sports is: "It's not fun anymore." Imagine what the game would look like if we all played with joy instead of pressure. Imagine if we coached with joy. Imagine if fun was one of our core values! We might just win more, too. Dale Carnegie wisely said, "People rarely succeed unless they have fun in what they are doing."

Did you know that the word fun *is never mentioned in the Bible?* But the concept of fun is unmistakable throughout—only God's version of fun is wrapped up in the superior word *joy*! Joy is the deep feeling of great pleasure, satisfaction, and happiness regardless of the circumstances. Joy is something we experience on the inside that overflows on the outside. We shouldn't be able to contain it. We were born to play, and when we play, there is joy and fun.

There's a great picture of overflowing joy in Acts 16. When Paul and Silas healed a girl of an evil spirit that allowed her to predict the future, her owners lost their ability to make money. So the crowd seized Paul and Silas, beat them severely, and threw them in prison. Chained and guarded closely, they clearly were not having fun. But they chose joy.

> *About midnight Paul and Silas were praying and singing hymns to God, and the other prisoners were listening to them. Suddenly there was such a violent earthquake that the foundations of the prison were shaken. At once all the prison doors flew open, and everybody's chains came loose.*
>
> ACTS 16:25–26

After witnessing this miracle, the guard asked what he had to do to be saved.

> *They replied, "Believe in the Lord Jesus, and you will be saved—you and your household."…Then immediately he and all his family were baptized…he was filled with joy because he had come to believe in God—he and his whole family.*
>
> VERSES 31–34 ABRIDGED

The guard literally threw a party. Now that *is* fun! And he had a lot to be joyful about.

Sometimes the Christian life feels a lot like competitive sports—like we've sucked the fun out of it. It's no wonder many want to quit. If we're going to make it for the long haul, we better make it fun. If we hate it, we may not stick to it. Devotions shouldn't be drudgery. We should look forward to church. And our joy should overflow—on the field, in the locker room, on the bus, in the classroom, and at home. Sports aren't a matter of life and death. They're meant to be enjoyed, not only by the fans and spectators, but by those who coach and *play the game.* We can create a culture of intensity and still have fun.

The Fun Factor is this: *if it's fun, it gets done!* And others are far more likely to join in. So let's make our faith fun again.

A 2009 study in Stockholm, Sweden, proved the Fun Factor by converting a set of stairs leading down to a subway to an actual working piano keyboard. Each step became one of the white or black keys on a piano so when you took a step, it played the note. At first, people were hesitant to step on it, but within two days, 66 percent of the people took the stairs (the hard way) instead of the escalator (the easy way) right next to it. Almost no one chose the stairs when they were just plain old stairs. But when they were transformed into something fun, people literally jumped for joy—all the way up the steps!

My mom used to ask me, "Are you happy?" When I said yes, she would say, "Then you better tell your face." Our joy should overflow into everything we do so others see it on our faces!

Our practices should have joy. Our games should be joyful. Our lives should be too, regardless of the external circumstances. Let God fill you with joy overflowing, because if it's fun, it gets done.

Be a GameChanger!

Live Intentionally. Maximize Relationships. Pass the Torch.

Live It

Do you have fun playing your sport? Or are you getting burned out? Explain.

Do you look forward to practice or dread it? Why?

Would you describe your relationship with Christ as "fun"? Why or why not?

Maximize It

Read 1 Peter 1:8; 3 John 1:4. Do you have that same sense of joy in knowing Jesus? In seeing others walk in the truth? Why or why not?

Read 2 Corinthians 7:4; James 1:2. What do these verses suggest about how we can respond even to adversity and trials?

Pass It

Grab a teammate and discuss the *WisdomWalks* principle—*If it's fun, it gets done.* What can you do to inject fun into your program so you play at your best and have fun doing it? Brainstorm ways to make the game fun again— to practice and to play.

My GamePlan

_____

_____

_____

_____

_____

_____

_____

_____

Father, thank You for being a God of joy! I know I'm far more likely to do the things I need to when they are fun. Please bring me joy as I seek You and spend time in Your Word. I pray that the joy inside me would overflow in all areas of my life, creating a culture of fun that others want to be around. Let me point them all to Jesus, the source of my joy! Amen.

13

THE LOVE WIN

Coaches love their players; players love each other.

Coaching is a profession of love. You can't coach people unless you love them.
EDDIE ROBINSON

On June 26, 2010, thousands gathered at a memorial service to honor the life of legendary coach John Wooden. He lived ninety-nine full years well, died well, and understood his eternal destiny. He once said, "There is only one kind of life that truly wins, and that is the one that places faith in the hands of the Savior."

In 2009, *Sporting News Magazine* made a list of the fifty greatest coaches of all time. It must have been an incredible challenge to narrow it down to fifty and nearly impossible to select the number-one coach—Coach Wooden. Why Wooden? Maybe it was because he'd won ten NCAA national championships at UCLA. Maybe it was because he was the coach that all the other coaches looked to as the benchmark of success. But I believe it was because of the heart of the man.

Wooden's purpose in coaching was to make not only better players but better people. He was committed to teaching, inspiring, and motivating people, and empowering his players to be the best men they could be. Wooden believed coaching should have a lasting impact that develops and instills habits and practices for life. For him, greatness was found in loving his players.

His coaching was marked with love and is reflected by these words by Oscar Hammerstein II:

A bell is no bell 'til you ring it.
A song is no song 'til you sing it.
And love in your heart wasn't put there to stay.
Love isn't love 'til you give it away.

Coach Wooden knew his number-one job was to love his players unconditionally. Love isn't usually found in most coaching job descriptions, but Bobby Dodd, former football coach at Georgia Tech, once said, "Either love your players or get out of coaching." When Joe Ehrmann, former NFL player for the Baltimore Colts, was coaching the Gilman High School football team, he would tell the players: *"Our job as coaches is to love you. Your job as players is to love each other."*

That's the Love Win. It's a powerful principle that can transform a team—and possibly the sports world! It's the missing ingredient.

When coaches love their players, they demonstrate it in the way they teach, the way they correct, the way they push. Coaches who love their players don't shame them in front of their teammates. They don't condemn publicly and tear down; they confront privately and build up. They care about what's going on in the classroom and at home. They work to understand the pressures their players are feeling off the field as well. They serve their players and step in to help in whatever way they can, because they are tuned into the needs and hurts of their players. They're intentional about modeling and building specific character qualities into the hearts of their players—integrity, perseverance, consistency, teamwork, and forgiveness. If coaches would coach their players the way Jesus loved His disciples, sports would be instantly impacted! The world of sports could be redeemed through transformed coaches and athletes.

My command is this: Love each other as I have loved you. Greater love has no one than this, that he lay down his life for his friends.... This is my command: Love each other.

JOHN 15:12–13, 17

Imagine what would happen if every coach followed the Love Win and could say, "My goal is to love my players!" Once coaches set the standard by loving their players, the players' number-one job is to love their teammates. When they create a culture of love, it replaces distrust, bitterness, envy, anger, and jealousy. Paul defines the Love Win for players in this way: "Love is patient, love is kind. It does not envy, it does not boast, it is not proud. It is not rude, it is not self-seeking, it is not easily angered, it keeps no record of wrongs. Love does not delight in evil but rejoices with the truth. It always protects, always trusts, always hopes, always perseveres" (1 Corinthians 13:4–7).

Players love each other by speaking words of encouragement. They believe the best in each other. They get excited when their teammates succeed and celebrate with them. They pick each other up when they are down and don't blame each other for mistakes. Instead of complaining about a lack of playing time, they continue to work hard, and everyone takes responsibility for their own effort. All negative talk and behind-the-scenes "locker room" talk that divides and discourages is shut down.

Love is the one thing that gets people's attention—especially when it's displayed in the arena of competition. It is a glimpse of the kingdom of God here on earth. Putting love into action is a picture of Jesus. When coaches love their players and players love each other, they are becoming more like Jesus. All relationships on a team must be rooted in love. If we make the Love Win our goal, we can show the world that sports can be different. Let the competition to live the Love Win begin!

Be a GameChanger!

Live Intentionally. Maximize Relationships. Pass the Torch.

Live It

How would you respond if you were given a title with the word *greatest* in it (for example, "Greatest Coach Ever" or "Greatest Athlete Ever")? Be honest. If you could be the greatest ever at something, what would it be? Why?

Do you see the Love Win lived out in sports today? If so, give a specific example.

Read 1 Corinthians 8:1; Philippians 1:9–11; 1 Thessalonians 3:12; 1 John 2:10. What do these verses say about love? How could such an attitude change your words and actions—on the field, at home, at church, in life in general?

Maximize It

How can coaches love their players? How can athletes love their teammates? List three specific ways for each.

Read Romans 12:9–21. Why is it hard to rejoice with others when they are rejoicing? Why is it hard to weep with those who are weeping?

How can you make the Love Win your goal? Explain.

Pass It

Grab a teammate and discuss the *WisdomWalks* principle: *Coaches love their players; players love each other.* Reflect on the past week. How have each of you reflected this principle in life on the field and in the locker room? How could the Love Win become a team goal? Brainstorm some specific ways.

My GamePlan

_____

_____

_____

_____

_____

_____

Lord, I love You, and that is much easier than loving people. It's difficult to love people because they let me down and disappoint me. But I ask You to give me a heart of love so that I will love unconditionally. I desire the Love Win in my life. Help me to love other competitors at full strength. In the name of Jesus I pray, amen.

14

THE LARRY PRINCIPLE

WisdomWalks Principle
Serving is leading.

Life's most urgent and persistent question is,
"What are you doing for others?"

DR. MARTIN LUTHER KING JR.

Larry, at only thirteen years old, made a significant impact on my life. It happened at a Fellowship of Christian Athletes camp, during a tradition that has played out at every FCA camp for more than fifty-five years. The last night features an open mic session when athletes come forward and share how camp has influenced their lives. It's the highlight of the entire week.

I'll never forget the FCA Leadership Camp I was directing several years ago when Larry got up to share at open mic night. After a terrific week of training middle school and high school students on how to impact their campus for Christ, it was now time to hear how God had worked in their hearts during the service projects, leadership workshops, hands-on training, inspiring speakers, and powerful worship that had marked the week.

Larry was a five-foot-tall seventh grader from inner-city Kansas City and a hit with the campers. He was funny, lovable, charming, and outspoken. His contagious laugh and raspy voice made Larry stand out from the others, and he became the camp favorite.

The open mic session had already gone thirty minutes too long when Larry stood to be the last in line to share. Larry was never short of words, but when he leaned into the microphone, he shared a single transformational leadership statement. His one sentence hit me between the eyes: "If you ain't serving, you ain't leading!"

Then he turned around, walked off the stage, and sat down. Larry, the Great Theologian, had spoken. I was in awe. I'd read hundreds of leadership books and articles, listened to tons of leadership talks and podcasts, written devotions about leadership, and I had just heard the ultimate leadership challenge—from a thirteen-year-old! And in seven words he'd communicated one of the most profound concepts I've ever heard on leadership.

That was a watershed moment for me. Larry's words still ring in my ears. His insight has changed the way I lead and serve. "If you ain't serving, you ain't leading!" has become my personal definition of leadership...all because of a seventh grader God used in my life.

It's all about serving, not leading. Everybody wants to be a leader, but no one (or very few) want to be a servant. As a result, whenever I speak at one of FCA's Leadership Camps, I usually say to the young leaders at the beginning of camp, "Welcome to Servant Camp!" We don't call them that in our marketing, because no one would show up! But Jesus says, "So the last will be first, and the first will be last" (Matthew 20:16 NLT).

When Billy Graham's late wife, Ruth, commented to the president of Wheaton College that the college was training leaders, he replied, "No, not leaders, but servants." All of us need to go into training to become servants, not leaders. Do you have a burning desire to serve with everything you have?

In 1 Peter 4:10–11 (NLT), the apostle Peter writes: "God has given each of you a gift from his great variety of spiritual gifts. Use them well to serve one another. Do you have the gift of speaking? Then speak as though God himself were speaking through you. Do you have the gift of helping others? Do it with all the strength and energy that God supplies. Then everything you do will bring glory to God through Jesus Christ"

It's hard to serve others in the arena of competition. But when it happens, the world takes notice. In 1976, at a Special Olympics track and field event in Spokane, Washington, one contestant took a tumble. Another athlete turned back to help the fallen one. Then, together, the two athletes crossed the finish line. I doubt there was a dry eye in the crowd watching that day. What a classic example of one competitor serving another during competition!

This type of serving comes from the heart. As competitors, we know all about passion. But do we have passion to serve? Do we hit the field or court and say, "How can I serve someone today at practice?" Samuel Chadwick nailed it when he wrote: "Spirit-filled souls are ablaze for God. They love with a love that glows. They serve with a faith that kindles. They serve with a devotion that consumes."

The end-result of our serving is for His glory. After we have served others, they should think, *God is good,* not, *You are good.* The purpose of serving is to lift the name of Jesus. Rick Warren says, "We serve God by serving others. The world defines greatness in terms of power, possessions, prestige, and position. In our self-serving culture with its me-first mentality, acting like a servant is not a popular concept." But when we serve, we represent to the world of sports what Jesus looks like.

Wisdom Walkers, let the Larry Principle burn in your heart: "If you ain't serving, you ain't leading!"

Be a GameChanger!

Live Intentionally. Maximize Relationships. Pass the Torch.

Live It

How would you describe your leadership style? Why? What would others say about it? Be bold enough to ask a couple of teammates or close friends what they think (and then shut your mouth and listen).

How does the Larry Principle impact you? How can you become a greater servant on your team, in your school, and with your family?

Read Mark 10:45; Luke 17:10; Galatians 5:13. Pray, asking God to reveal opportunities to serve your teammates.

Maximize It

Read John 13:1–15. How did Jesus serve? How can you serve like Jesus? What does it mean for you to wash others' feet?

How can you serve others when competing? Be specific.

If you had been running in that 1976 Special Olympics event, would you have gone back to help the athlete who fell? Why or why not?

Pass It

Grab a teammate and discuss the *WisdomWalks* principle: *Serving is leading.* How can you individually create a culture of serving on your team? Brainstorm specific ways you could serve other teammates and coaches.

My GamePlan

_____

_____

_____

_____

_____

_____

_____

_____

_____

_____

Father, I ask for a heart to serve—with a pure heart. Forgive me for the times I serve with the wrong motive. Teach me how to serve others at full strength. I have teammates who need to see Jesus through my serving. It's an incredible responsibility, but I know You will help me as I remain faithful. My desire is to serve with a supernatural power, a clear purpose, a specific plan, and a consuming passion. Use me for Your kingdom work. Amen.

15

SUPERSIZE ME

WisdomWalks Principle
Toxic material will make you sick.

One leak will sink a ship. One sin will destroy a sinner.
JOHN BUNYAN, *THE PILGRIM'S PROGRESS*

For thirty days—three meals a day—Morgan Spurlock ate nothing but McDonald's. Then he produced a documentary called *Super Size Me* that tracked his every move. He only supersized when asked, tried everything on the menu at least once, and had a doctor monitor his health throughout. About halfway through, Spurlock began to feel sick, and by the end his health had deteriorated significantly. He gained twenty-four pounds, his body-fat percentage doubled, his cholesterol went up sixty-five points, and he experienced huge mood swings, cravings, and headaches. His energy level plunged, and he even got depressed. He was a "train wreck" in just thirty days. Worst of all, it took him fourteen months to undo the damage done in just thirty days.

I used to have a problem with fast food. In fact, my whole family did. We were running so hard from one activity to the next and from field to field that we began stopping in at the most convenient fast food restaurants we could find. At the time, we didn't think it was a problem. But when I came home one day and saw several bags of garbage in my wife's van and then the same in my own car, I was convicted. I knew this was not God's best for my family. And, as the operator of a wellness center, I knew I had an integrity problem as well. That moment marked one of the last times we ate fast food.

When we expose ourselves to toxic material, we'll eventually get sick. Proverbs 25:26 (NLT) says, "If the godly give in to the wicked, it's like polluting a fountain or muddying a spring." God has designed us as vessels of living water that refreshes others, but when we allow toxic material to enter, we become morally muddy and personally polluted. Not only do we get sick; we can make others sick as well.

Toxic material is anything poisonous and capable of causing sickness or death. It's a synonym for good old-fashioned sin. Toxic material could be things we see, words we say, stuff we crave, or even people. It can do three things inside us. First Corinthians 5:6–7 cautions, "A little yeast *works its way through the whole batch* of dough" (emphasis added); a small compromise and exposure to toxic material ends up spreading. Hebrews 12:1 says sin tangles us up. It's literally like getting caught in a spider's web. Ephesians 4:27 warns us not to give the Enemy a "foothold" from which he can launch further attacks.

There are three key sources of toxic material—words, friends, and stuff.

Toxic words can be ones said or thought. Words have the power of life and death. Reckless words pierce like a sword. Harsh words stir up conflict. Criticism can crush our spirit. And words that are spoken often stay with us for years. Some words we never forget. But sometimes the harshest words are the ones we think and say to ourselves—words like *I can't, I'm not good enough,* and *It'll never work.* I call that "stinkin' thinkin.'" Over time, negative and defeated thinking spreads and takes over. In competition, you'll defeat yourself with your thoughts and words before your opponent even makes a play. That's because your words reveal your true belief, and it's impossible to win when you don't believe you can. Then when a coach calls you out with crushing criticism in front of your teammates, it destroys your desire to play at your best.

Toxic friends are false friends. They have no desire to help you become the man or woman God has made you to be. In fact, misery loves company, and bad company corrupts good morals (1 Corinthians 15:33). Toxic friends are Complainers, Criticizers, or Tempters. Complainers never have anything positive to say; the glass of life is always half empty. They see the problem instead of the potential and the obstacle instead of the opportunity. Criticizers find all your faults and drag you down. In the locker room, those who complain and criticize kill the unity and spirit of the team. Tempters always push you to do things you have decided not to do—alcohol, sex, you name it. Like it or not, toxic teammates and friends will tear you down.

Toxic stuff looks good but goes bad. We can expose ourselves to toxic stuff on TV, the Internet, movies, and even our phones. It's available 24/7. While shopping we may be tempted to think that we "need" to buy something now. Toxic stuff could even be unhealthy food that compromises our health. Searching for substitutes to satisfy our cravings will only make us sick. Toxic stuff always overpromises and under-delivers.

We are called to live a life worthy of the Lord. "Since we have these promises, dear friends, let us purify ourselves from everything that contaminates body and spirit, perfecting holiness out of reverence for God" (2 Corinthians 7:1).

Isn't it time to cut off the source that is making you sick? Let God reveal the toxic material in your life—and get clean!

Be a GameChanger!

Live Intentionally. Maximize Relationships. Pass the Torch.

Live It

Read Proverbs 12:18; 13:20; 1 John 2:15–17. What do these verses say about toxic words, friends, and stuff?

Is there evidence of toxic words of criticism, complaining, blaming, and negativity on your team? In the locker room? On the field?

What toxic material have you been exposed to this week? What effect has it had on your heart? How does it affect your attitude toward your teammates and coaches? Does it weigh you down? How?

What is the biggest source of toxic material for you? Why?

Maximize It

Read 2 Corinthians 7:1. What are some specific ways we can purify ourselves from toxic material? How do we cut off the source?

Read Acts 3:19; James 5:16. Why is confession and repentance the best way to remove the effects of toxic material? What does confession and repentance lead to?

Read Proverbs 4:23–27; 2 Corinthians 10:5; Philippians 4:8. Why is it so important to guard our hearts and minds? If we do, what does it do for our eyes, mouth, and feet?

Pass It

Grab a teammate and discuss the *WisdomWalks* principle: *Toxic material will make you sick.* What toxic material has the worst effect on you and your teammates? Find ways to remove it and replace it with things that bring life in the locker room, on the field, in your home, and in your heart.

My GamePlan

_____

_____

_____

_____

_____

_____

_____

_____

Father, I know I've exposed myself to toxic material. It's working its way into my life, tangling me up, and tearing me down. Search my heart and reveal to me specific toxic material that needs to go. I want to be clean and refreshed by the work of Your Holy Spirit. Please forgive me for the things I have done and make me healthy again. Amen.

16

DON'T BE STUPID

WisdomWalks Principle
Two are better than one.

*Humbling yourself by letting others into your life and allowing
them to help you and hold you accountable will release the sanctifying,
transforming grace of God in your life.*
NANCY LEIGH DeMOSS

Go wherever you want, whenever you want! It was a one-of-a-kind wristband. My hometown Kansas City Royals were playing against the famous New York Yankees, and when a friend gave me the All-Access wristband, I was fired up. And I mean *all access!* On the field for batting practice, in the dugout, or in the locker room—I could go wherever I wanted. All I had to do was lift my arm with my All-Access wristband, and they let me in. There was nothing off-limits. I was granted permission to wander and explore.

Who has the all-access wristband in your life? We often talk about God having all access to our lives, and yes, the Lord should have all access. When we surrender our lives to Jesus Christ, He has permission to wander, explore, and enter any room of our hearts. Nothing is off-limits. However, it's another thing when we talk about another human being having all access. Do you have at least one trusted friend who has all access in your life?

We all need at least one trusted friend to share our hearts with—someone who has the green light to the door of our life, someone with whom no subject is out of bounds or off-limits. This is someone who lifts us up when we stumble and holds us down when we stray. They are absolutely, totally committed to our spiritual, physical, mental, and emotional success. For the WisdomWalker, we call this trusted friend a Warrior, a key part of our Dream Team.

But accountability never works when it's demanding. There can be no judgment or condemnation, only tough love and compassion; the real work is done by the Holy Spirit—and we are not Him! The all-access pass only works when you allow access. Then things once hidden can be exposed so God can deal with the sin and heal us.

As Charles R. Swindoll says, "Accountability includes opening one's life to a few carefully selected, trusted, loyal confidants who speak the truth—who have the right to examine, to question, to appraise, and to give counsel."

What should you look for in an all-access-pass friend? This trusted friend needs to be someone who will fight for you—and you're willing to do the same for them.

These are the kinds of friends who will hold you accountable in the areas of purity, faith, and integrity and will fight for these things in their own lives. They don't walk away when things get tough or when you reveal the truth about what's really going on inside. Accountability is more than just asking tough questions. It's staying engaged and involved in the messy areas of struggle until victory is won.

All of us are one step away from making a stupid decision. All-access-pass friends help create moral margin and keep us at a safer distance from stupid. They expand our safety zone.

But there's something in each of us that says we can't stand alone; we don't need others. After all, we're competitors. We do things by ourselves. We're self-disciplined. We're independent. I once heard an athlete say, "We would have a great team except for all my teammates!" Yes, we talk team, but we value self. And when push comes to shove, we honor self over team.

Don't fall into that trap of isolation. There is a great African proverb that states, "If you want to go fast, go alone. If you want to go far, go together." *To finish the race of faith, we must run together.*

Isolation is the Christian's silent enemy. But don't get solitude and silence (two powerful spiritual disciplines) mixed up with isolation. Isolation is pulling away and saying, "I can live out my faith on my own, and I don't need anyone to help me." There is pride in isolation. We begin to think we can live our faith through our own power. Once we distance ourselves from those who know us best, changes begin taking place in the absence of accountability. Isolation makes people believe that sin can be committed without consequences.

Additionally, isolation makes us think that we are the only people wrestling with a particular sin, problem, difficulty, or addiction. We begin to believe that no one else will understand us, so why should we open up and seek help? We think that if we keep a lid on our problems, we will contain them.

Accountability is a nonnegotiable in the Christian life. For twenty years, I have had at least one Warrior I meet with on a weekly basis—someone who asks me tough questions. Accountability has allowed me to live for Christ with greater purity and passion. Truthfully speaking, I don't know if I could survive without the people who hold me accountable.

Simply stated, the banana separated from the bunch gets peeled first. So don't be stupid. Don't think you can live for Christ without being connected. The Christian life is intended to be lived as a team sport. Get a Warrior or two. Two are better than one.

Be a GameChanger!

Live Intentionally. Maximize Relationships. Pass the Torch.

Live It

To you, is the Christian life more of an individual thing or a team thing? Explain.

Do you—or have you ever had—a Warrior? How have others helped you in your spiritual journey? What impact has it made in your life?

Read Romans 15:1–2; Ephesians 4:25; Hebrews 3:13; James 5:16. What do these verses say about faithful friends and authentic accountability? What one or two friends could become that for you—and you for them? What could an accountability relationship with that friend or friends look like?

Maximize It

Read 1 Samuel 18:1–3; 20:16–17. What was special about David and Jonathan's relationship? Why is love so important in a Warrior relationship?

What other examples from the Bible come to mind when thinking about a lack of accountability? As an athlete, why is isolation so easy and accountability so hard?

Why is there power in confessing sin to another person? How does it bring freedom?

Pass It

Grab a teammate and discuss the *WisdomWalks* principle: *Two are better than one.* When have each of you experienced authentic accountability? How can accountability among teammates make your team stronger?

My GamePlan

_____

_____

_____

_____

_____

_____

_____

Father God, I want to finish the race of faith well. I don't want to drop out or even stumble over the finish line. My desire is to run with endurance, keeping my eyes fixed on You! I need friends in my life to help me finish strong, and I want to help them finish strong. I ask for strength to break free from the sin of isolation and secrecy. Help me to be open and transparent with at least one other believer. I don't want to live out my faith alone anymore. In Jesus' name, amen.

17

PROTECT THIS HOUSE

WisdomWalks Principle
If you don't fight, you're dead meat.

The more you sweat in practice, the less you bleed in battle.
US NAVY SEALS

During my senior year high school basketball season, we were winning our division and on our way to the Section V playoffs when we faced an inferior opponent, a team with only two wins that promised to be an "easy win." It was a home game, giving us an even bigger advantage. We were loose all week in practice and, in hindsight, lacked intensity. We were looking past this game to our first playoff clash. That proved to be a mistake. We got beat by an inferior team on our home court. It was embarrassing. By the time we started to play with our characteristic focus, intensity, and teamwork, it was too late. We had failed to "protect our house."

We ended up using that game as a reminder to never let our guard down. We considered our opponent inferior and went in unprepared for battle. We were unaware that, to them, this game was the "championship." They were gunning for us; they wanted to take us down and salvage their season. And they had changed their defensive scheme and caught us sleeping. Thankfully, that game fueled our focus for the future; we went on to win the Section V Championship and advanced to the New York State tournament. But it could have derailed us.

I was reminded of that season recently when the Under Armour commercial blasted the question, "Will you protect this house?" Every competitor responded, "I will. I will. I will." We love the battle. We love the competition. And to get ready for it, we put in hours of training and practice. We prepare our bodies and our minds to know what to expect. On the field or court, we contest every point. We stand our ground. We take our shots. We "man up." There's no backing down or giving in. But if we let our guard down for even one game, we can get beat.

Life is no different. *We have two enemies—the Inside Enemy and the Outside Enemy.* Unfortunately, many of us don't view life as a battle. We think we're on a vacation cruise ship instead of a battleship. As a result, we don't approach challenges with that competitor's mind-set or from a spiritual perspective. We are often unaware of the spiritual battle that rages in us and around us. Or we consider the Enemy inferior and look past him. As a result, we are unprepared to "protect this house."

The Inside Enemy includes the *lust of the flesh.* Our "flesh" wants what it wants when it wants it; you can think of it as cravings. Paul describes our internal struggle in Romans 7:21: "When I want to do good, evil is right there with me." The Spirit always wars against our self. And our old nature always has a craving for sin. God never tempts us; instead we are tempted by our old nature.

The temptations in your life are no different from what others experience. And God is faithful. He will not allow the temptation to be more than you can stand. When you are tempted, he will show you a way out so that you can endure.

1 Corinthians 10:13 nlt

The Outside Enemy includes the lies of the Devil and the lure of the world. Our spiritual adversary is fierce, and his goal is to steal, kill, and destroy (1 Peter 5:8). So…

Don't believe everything you feel. When we're prepared to "protect this house," we see the temptations coming and either take our stand or simply walk away. When we're unprepared, we get beaten by an inferior opponent. But God always gives us a way out.

Don't believe everything you think. When you're lonely, he'll tell you the lie that God has left you. When you're discouraged or down, he'll tell you you're worth nothing.

Don't believe everything you see. The lure of the world is powerful, and the Devil knows it. That's why he spends so much time tempting us with physical pleasure, material stuff, awards, and recognition.

We have everything we need to overcome the Inside Enemy and the Outside Enemy. God gives us two primary weapons—the same ones Jesus used to fight with and win: prayer and the Word of God. When the Devil tempted Jesus, Jesus always responded with Scripture. And when Jesus was teaching His followers, He regularly went away to pray in solitude.

Second Corinthians 10:4 says, "The weapons we fight with are not the weapons of the world. On the contrary, they have divine power to demolish strongholds."

If you don't fight, you're dead meat. You must protect your body, mind, and soul by using the Word and being devoted to prayer. So prepare for the battle for your heart like you prepare for the battle on the field; it's time to fight to protect this house. And may you say wholeheartedly, "I will. I will. I will!"

Be a GameChanger!

Live Intentionally. Maximize Relationships. Pass the Torch.

Live It

Read James 1:13–14. What are some of the things that tempt you the most? Why do they draw you?

Read John 10:10; 1 Peter 5:8. Is our Outside Enemy passive or active? What is his purpose? How can you prepare to stand against this type of enemy?

Maximize It

Read 1 Corinthians 10:13; 1 John 4:4. What do these verses say about the strength within you and your ability to escape temptation?

Read Proverbs 4:23; James 4:7. What are specific ways you can guard your heart and resist the Devil?

Read 2 Corinthians 10:3–5; Ephesians 6:10–18. What are the weapons you can use to fight? How can God's Word help you fight—and win? Pick one verse this week to memorize as you get ready to fight.

Pass It

Grab a teammate and discuss the *WisdomWalks* principle: *If you don't fight, you're dead meat.* What inside temptations are you currently facing? What ones have you faced in the past? Identify ways the Outside Enemy may be trying to divide or distract your team. Brainstorm specifics to "protect this house" and encourage others to stand strong.

My GamePlan

_____

_____

_____

_____

_____

_____

_____

_____

Father, I know that, just like in competition, I face opponents in life. Help me to be ready to fight the battle against the Inside Enemy—the lusts of the flesh—and the Outside Enemy—the lies of the Devil and the lure of the world. I know I am more than a conqueror in Christ and that, with every temptation, You give me a way out. Give me the wisdom I need to flee temptations, and equip me through Your Word to fight! Amen.

18

THIS IS A BIBLE

WisdomWalks Principle
Engage God, no matter what.

*It is far better to begin with God—to see His face first,
to get my soul near Him before it is near another.*
ROBERT MURRAY M'CHEYNE

oach Buckley's football practices were brutal. I was only eleven, but I still remember them to be grueling, agonizing, and dreadful. The trademark practices had tons of running and repetitive drills, all without scrimmaging! Many players wouldn't make it through the practices without losing their lunch, and many of them quit. Even my best friend left the team; his parents pulled him. But, even though the sacrifice was great, the return was sweet. We earned a perfect season, in which no team even scored on us! The Braddock Road Sharks brought fear to all eleven-year-olds who dared to play football.

Our practices were not marked by complexity but by simplicity. Drills, drills, and more drills. We went over the basics in every practice. Coach Buckley stressed the fundamentals of the game and the fundamentals of each position. Those fundamentals were the key to our success.

Great coaches always stress the basics. They understand that focusing on the essentials makes their players compete at their highest level. Coaches who assume that fundamentals don't need to be stressed throughout the year are usually looking for a new job at the end of the season.

If fundamentals are the key to success on sports teams, then what would be the fundamentals of being on God's team? What are the basics that our Head Coach, Jesus Christ, would want us to focus on?

In 1959, legendary football coach Vince Lombardi, while holding a football in front of him, said to his Green Bay Packers: "Let's start at the beginning. This is a football." Could it be any more basic than that? In the same way, I think Jesus stands up in front of us each day and holds up the Word of God and says, "This is a Bible."

Over the next eight years, Coach Lombardi transformed the Packers program by sticking to the basics. They were in a class by themselves, winning six divisional and five NFL championships and achieving two Super Bowl victories.

But Jesus Christ desires to transform your life in an even greater way than that! All it takes is following His direction. So start taking in the Word of God. Read through the Bible, and it will change you. Time after time in my life, I've realized anew that spiritual victory is directly related to time spent in His Word. Psalm 119:147 reminds me of the importance of connecting with the Lord: "I rise before dawn and cry for help; I have put my hope in your word." Position yourself to let Him speak into your life.

In Mark 1:35, we learn one of Jesus' keys to success. *It was fundamental for Jesus to engage with His Father every day. It was not an option. It was a must.* Mark writes:

> *Very early in the morning, while it was still dark, Jesus got up, left the house and went off to a solitary place, where he prayed.*

It's a battle every day to pick up the Bible when we've got so much on our to-do lists. That's because our Enemy doesn't want us to spend time daily in the Word. He knows that if we do, our lives will be transformed... and others' lives will be transformed. And he'll do anything to prevent that from happening. So he'll throw everything he can at us to prevent us from cracking open the Book of Truth.

But if you want clarity and spiritual success in your life, start with the Word of God. Focus on the spiritual fundamentals. Oswald Chambers said, "Simplicity is the secret of seeing things clearly." Get going and dive in! Just you and the Bible. Open it, read it, study it, meditate on it, and linger in it. Let it soak into you!

So let's start from the beginning—"This is a Bible."

Step 1: Grab a Bible.

Step 2: Open it.

Step 3: Read it.

Step 4: Experience it for yourself.

Be a GameChanger!

Live Intentionally. Maximize Relationships. Pass the Torch.

Live It

As an athlete or coach, you're busy. Your time is limited. But what things *really* keep you from making a priority of reading the Word of God on a daily basis? List them.

How can you make sure those things do not become barriers? Write a solution for each.

Read Psalm 1:2–3; 119:49–56; Matthew 6:6; 1 Timothy 6:11–12. What do these verses say about the importance of spending time with God? And the benefits of doing so?

Maximize It

What are some other spiritual fundamentals? How can you integrate them into your life, your competition, and your team?

What is the best time of day for you to pick up the Bible? Why?

How can you reprioritize your day so that you spend time alone with God on a daily basis?

Pass It

Grab a teammate and discuss the *WisdomWalks* principle: *Engage God, no matter what.* If the success of your team were based on your discipline of engaging God daily and not the talent of your teammates and coaches, how successful would your team be? How could engaging with God each day transform your team and teammates?

My GamePlan

_____

_____

_____

_____

_____

_____

_____

_____

_____

_____

_____

_____

Father God, I ask You to make it plain and simple to me. Show me how much I need the basics in my life. Teach me the simplicity of picking up Your Word. May the act of picking up the Bible, reading it, and meditating on it change me to be more like You. May I experience You in a fresh new way today because of my time in the Bible. Thank You, Jesus, for Your instructions and commands. They are sweet to my soul. In Your name, amen.

19

BRAVEHEART

WisdomWalks Principle
Faith overcomes fear.

*Fear will always knock on your door. Just don't let it in.
Learn to trust more and fear less.*

MAX LUCADO

Recently, two of my sons were playing in a lacrosse tournament that attracted some of the top club teams from across the country. Their teams were playing well and had advanced to the semifinal round. Incredibly, the semifinal game ended in a tie. They had battled for forty minutes without a winner! So, to determine which team would advance, each team sent just two players onto the field. They put their goalie in the net and had their best player head out to midfield for the face-off.

This tiebreaker is called *Braveheart*. It's sudden death—first one to score wins. A couple of the boys immediately told the coach they wanted the ball. They wanted to be the one on the field with the game on the line. And there's no question—these young men indeed had brave hearts. They were fearless. Or at least their courage helped them overcome their fear. These boys battled, and the game was over in less than thirty seconds.

On the field, when athletes play without fear, they play at their best. When they're afraid to make mistakes, they make mistakes. And they don't end up in the right place at the right time on the field.

That day, not everybody stepped up. Would you have?

Do you live your life with a brave heart? Do you want the ball with the game on the line? Are you fearless? Or do you shrink back? Do you care more about what people will think if you take a stand for your faith, or are you content with living to please God regardless of the cost? Will you share truth with a teammate or coach? Will you encourage friends to seek God and His wisdom for the problems they face? Will you overcome your fear of entering the conversation and revealing your deepest held beliefs? Do you want the ball? Do you?

We all share common fears. Many of us have a fear of failure. But many of us are equally afraid of being rejected or not fitting in. Others are afraid of feeling stupid or not knowing enough to defend their point. And most of us are afraid to speak into anyone's life because after all, "Who are we?" We don't have it all together either! So we stay quiet even though God is nudging us to get in the game, ask for the ball, and make a play.

All of us have heard the question, "If you could do anything in life and you knew you wouldn't fail, what would you do?" That question is easy to answer. I can find twenty things I'd do if I knew I wouldn't fail!

What if we tried to answer this question instead: "If you could do something really important in life, but you knew failure and embarrassment were very real possibilities, what would you do?"

Now *that* takes courage. And risk. And faith.

But fear paralyzes. It prevents us from doing the difficult things God asks us to do. It prevents us from taking risks—unless we are willing to let faith overcome fear.

Do you play to win, or not to lose? When we let fear reign, we play it safe. We start to doubt ourselves. Instead of going for it and playing to win, we play not to lose. We see it all the time—when teams get a lead, they stop doing the things that got them the lead and they try to "hold on for dear life." Why? Because we become afraid of making a mistake that might lose the game. We play scared and tentative. Nobody wants to be the one who blows it. But when we try not to lose, we lose. When we get behind, we let it rip—after all, what do we have to lose? And that belief fuels momentum and freedom on the field. When faith overcomes fear of failure, we play with freedom. We've got to play to win at all times.

Do you see challenge or God's capabilities? The Bible is full of stories of faith overcoming fear. And God regularly puts us in situations where we are in over our heads so we have to depend on Him.

In 1 Samuel 17, David, a teenager, faced down Goliath while the entire army of God looked on from the sidelines. His faith overcame the nation's fear.

In Judges 6, God grew Gideon's faith by *reducing* his army from 32,000 men to 300 to fight an enemy that would number over 100,000. And the faith of the nation was strengthened.

In the book of Esther, Esther risked her life to stand up to the king and saved Mordecai and the Jewish people.

In Numbers 13, Caleb was the only one of twelve spies who told Moses they could possess the Promised Land. He wanted the ball!

Have I not commanded you? Be strong and courageous. Do not be terrified; do not be discouraged, for the LORD your God will be with you wherever you go.

JOSHUA 1:9

Being courageous doesn't mean having no fear. It means taking action by faith in the face of fear.

No matter what challenge you are facing today, have a brave heart. Take a risk. Attempt something important for God. Ask for the ball. Let *faith overcome fear*. And remember, God is with you wherever you go.

Be a GameChanger!

Live Intentionally. Maximize Relationships. Pass the Torch.

Live It

Would you describe yourself as fearful or fearless in the sports arena? Would others describe you as tentative or all-out? Why?

When are you most anxious or fearful? Have you ever been afraid to make a mistake that could cost you the game? Explain.

Do you play with the faith to win or with fear of losing? Give an example.

Maximize It

Read Ephesians 6:19–20. When it comes to expressing your faith, how can this prayer give you courage?

How could you communicate fearlessly to others what God has done in your life? What might you say?

Read Psalm 20:7; John 14:26–27. What does Jesus tell us He gives us when we trust Him?

Do you tend to see the challenge of the competition or the capability of God? Explain.

Pass It

Grab a teammate and discuss the *WisdomWalks* principle: *Faith overcomes fear.* Ask, "Have you ever been afraid to talk about your faith?" Share a personal story of when you played with fear and when you overcame fear. Pray that everyone on your team would compete courageously without the fear of failure.

My GamePlan

_____

_____

_____

_____

_____

Father, help me focus on Your capabilities instead of the challenge in front of me. Develop in me the faith of David, Gideon, Esther, and Caleb. Help me to be strong and courageous even when I feel afraid and the situation seems impossible. Give me a boldness to tell others about the great things You are doing inside me. Change me from the inside out. Grant me Your power and strength. Amen.

20

BLOCKER OR BUILDER?

WisdomWalks Principle
Humility unlocks greatness in others.

Before you are a leader, success is all about growing yourself.
When you become a leader, success is all about growing others.
JACK WELCH

Coach Scott was a great offensive line football coach. As a ten-year-old aspiring right guard, I learned from him the basics to being a great blocker: elbows up and out with hands tucked in. It was the "old school" way to block, which didn't involve the use of hands—blockers would just stick their elbows way out so the defensive player couldn't get by. For me, a good game required making sure no one ever got around me and never got a tackle—not exactly a simple job. It took an incredible amount of work and effort to keep others from advancing toward the ball.

Blockers are everywhere in life—on our sports teams, in our classes, at our jobs, in our homes, and at our churches. Elbows up and out, they try their hardest to prevent others from getting around them. It's hard to be around them and serve under them because they're selfish, prideful, controlling people. They might say they care, but the proof is in how they put a lid over us and prevent us from moving forward. In reality, all of us have a blocker mind-set to some degree. It comes so naturally to look after our own interests. That's why we should constantly examine our own hearts for the blocker mentality.

There are Ten Blocker Commandments that outline the way blockers lead and how they treat others.

1. Blockers keep others from reaching their potential.
2. Blockers cannot celebrate the success of others.
3. Blockers look at life through the "me" lens, not the "we" lens.
4. Blockers criticize easily and can't praise others.

5. Blockers use the power given to them to advance themselves, not others.
6. Blockers fear that others will get credit for their accomplishments.
7. Blockers are threatened by people who are more gifted.
8. Blockers are insecure in who they are and in their giftedness.
9. Blockers do not recognize themselves as preventers, only as protectors who think they know what is best for others.
10. Blockers lead out of fear, pride, and control.

Instead of being blockers, let's choose to be builders. We can assist others in reaching their potential on and off the field of competition. Christ wants us to serve, bless, praise, encourage, and love others, doing whatever we can to see their gifts fully used for the kingdom of God.

But unlocking greatness in others only comes from a humble spirit. When you build others up, you have the incredible opportunity to become part of God's plan to help people release their potential. You get to experience God's work—through you!

As spiritual builders, we need to focus on helping athletes and coaches reach greatness. But we can only do that if we first lead and serve out of a humble heart. First Peter 5:5 (NIV, 2011) says, "In the same way, you who are younger, submit yourselves to your elders. All of you, clothe yourselves with humility toward one another, because, 'God opposes the proud but shows favor to the humble.'" And what is humility? Simply put, a proper view of oneself. It's not thinking more of yourself or less of yourself than who you are in Christ. Paul encourages us to have a sober self-assessment: "Don't think you are better than you really are. Be honest in your evaluation of yourselves, measuring yourselves by the faith God has given us." (Romans 12:3 NLT).

Yes, it is difficult to see people advance if it means that you won't. But the Lord can supernaturally change you so that you not only celebrate their success but cheer for them as they fly past you!

Builders know who they are in Christ and find their identity in Him. Blockers lead out of insecurity and find their identity in their position and performance. Builders know their strengths and weaknesses. They have a proper understanding of their giftedness. Blockers go out of their way to portray their own strength and rely on themselves alone.

If you are a builder, keep on doing what you're doing!

If you're a blocker, there is hope for you. Converting from being a blocker to a builder means emptying ourselves of pride and selfishness. It means adopting the kingdom-of-God mentality that we're all in life together. It means viewing our lives with a proper perspective and allowing God to transform us, through the power of His Holy Spirit, into a builder.

So I challenge you: tackle the blocker mentality and become a builder. Every team needs builders. Your humility will unlock greatness in others and build up the entire team.

Be a GameChanger!

Live Intentionally. Maximize Relationships. Pass the Torch.

Live It

Think of the blockers and builders in your life. What emotions do each prompt? What actions and attitudes make the difference?

What about you? Do you tend to be a builder or a blocker? Explain, using a specific example or two.

Read Proverbs 15:33; Micah 6:8; Philippians 2:3; James 4:10. What do these verses reveal about blocking and building? How do they encourage you to become a builder?

Maximize It

Which of the Ten Blocker Commandments do you struggle with the most? Why?

Think of two or three of your own Builder Commandments and write them down.

Read Romans 12:3. How can the Lord help you develop a builder mind-set? How could others help you become a humble competitor?

Who are you blocking right now? How might you start building that person instead?

Pass It

Grab a teammate and discuss the *WisdomWalks* principle: *Humility unlocks greatness in others.* How might your humility impact your teammates? Brainstorm specific ways to build teammates and coaches.

My GamePlan

_____

_____

_____

_____

_____

_____

_____

Father, it's so easy for me to be a blocker, but I desire to be a builder. Help me break out of my blocker attitude. I confess my pride. Replace it with humility. May I be a builder who serves others and loves them as only You can. Teach me to celebrate the victories of others. Show me how to assist them in reaching greatness. In the name of Jesus I pray, amen.

21

FIRED UP

WisdomWalks Principle
Character is formed in the fire.

*Every trial weathered with the right spirit
makes a soul nobler and stronger than it was before.*
JAMES BUCKHAM

Cut from the team. Blown-out knee senior year. Lost the state title. Playing time reduced. Made a mistake that cost the team a win…. All of these things are considered tough trials for competitors. Add to that academic pressure or conflict at home, and you can feel overwhelmed. When you're in the middle of it, it can feel like crisis-level kind of stuff. But the fire can be even more intense. Unexpected cancer. Lost loved one. Divorce. You know—life-altering kinds of trials.

My family recently experienced this kind of fire when we got a call from the doctor saying that my wife had the same kind of cancer that had ended her father's life at the age of thirty-nine. Only my wife's situation was worse—following surgery, it had spread to the liver. To say we were "going through the fire" would be right on target. We felt intense and growing pressure to maintain our everyday commitments (work, kids' school, sports, and activities), search for a solution, and cover the mounting medical obligations. We were definitely feeling the heat, and it tested our faith.

Character is uncovered in crisis and formed in the fire. It will be *revealed* and *refined*. When we are squeezed, what comes out shows us what's inside. And it gives us a chance to let God change us, especially when we don't like what we see.

In Daniel 3, we read the account of how Shadrach, Meshach, and Abednego faced one of the hottest trials in history. When they refused to bow down and worship a false god, they were literally thrown into the fiery furnace.

"If we are thrown into the blazing furnace, the God we serve is able to

save us from it…. But even if he does not, we want you to know, O king, that we will not serve your gods or worship the image of gold you have set up."…Then Nebuchadnezzar ordered the furnace heated seven times hotter than usual and commanded some of the strongest soldiers in his army to…throw them into the blazing furnace.

DANIEL 3:16–20 ABRIDGED

Adversity brings opportunity. The "Big Three," as I call them, faced a life-and-death situation. When they took their stand and fell into the fire, the soldiers who threw them in were killed instantly. But the Big Three were unharmed. And they were not alone; they were protected by an angel of God. Some believe it may have been the pre-incarnate Christ Jesus Himself. The Big Three were willing to trust God no matter what—whether they were delivered *from* danger or delivered *through* it.

Testing produces testimonies. When the king saw the unwavering faith and courage of these men and then witnessed this great miracle, he immediately gave praise to the one true God and recognized that "no other god can save in this way" (verse 29). When others see how we persevere and trust, they believe. I believe not only that everything happens *for a reason*, but that everything happens *for us to reason*.

In order for God to truly transform us, it takes time, pressure, and heat. He forms our character the same way He forms diamonds. The word *diamond* comes from the Greek word *adamas*, which means "invincible" or "unconquerable." It is formed from a single element, carbon. It takes not only time but extreme heat and pressure to transform carbon into a diamond. When carbon is forced to go deeper beneath the surface of the earth (100 miles down), it encounters extreme temperatures (2,200 degrees Fahrenheit) and pressure (725,000 pounds per square inch). Those extreme conditions make diamonds. And when the carbon rises again to the surface, it displays the brilliance of the light.

God uses trials to make us unshakable and Him unmistakable. Let the fire do its work. Carbon is common. Anybody can avoid adversity or tackle trials on his or her own and remain ordinary. But diamonds are uncommon. God wants to produce the extraordinary out of your adversity, and He will never leave your side.

The more "heat and pressure" we feel, the more "heart and presence" of God we experience. There is always purpose in pain. In 2 Corinthians 1:3–6 we are told that God comforts us so we can comfort others. When you face trials, you can do it with joy, expecting that God will use every piece of the pressure and pain to produce perseverance and maturity.

During my wife's battle with cancer, my family began to view it as a gift of sorts, because it radically deepened our faith and our enjoyment of the little things in life. We were able to fully place our trust in Him—no matter what. And by the miraculous grace of God, my wife has overcome cancer and remains cancer-free.

As competitors, we know that every season brings adversity—injuries, setbacks, disappointments. Sometimes the challenge is on the field; sometimes it's off. We need to see it for what it is: an opportunity to grow and be changed. God will make us complete, expand our faith, and bring glory to His name. Let your character be formed in the fire.

Be a GameChanger!

Live Intentionally. Maximize Relationships. Pass the Torch.

Live It

What adversities or trials have tested your faith? And what were the results?

What is your typical "first" response when you are put in the fire? Excitement for the opportunity, frustration, anger…something else? (Be honest.) How can looking at them as a gift change your perspective?

Read 1 Peter 4:12–16. Why are we often surprised when trials and suffering come? Why are we able to rejoice?

Maximize It

Read 2 Corinthians 1:3–6. What are the purposes of the pain we suffer in this life?

Read Proverbs 17:17; Luke 22:28. Why is it important to have others walk with you through your trials? Who are the friends who would be at your side? List them here.

Read James 1:2–4. How do trials change us?

Read Romans 8:29; 2 Peter 2:9. What do these verses reveal about the power and presence of God and what His ultimate goal is for us?

Pass It

Grab a teammate and discuss the *WisdomWalks* principle: *Character is formed in the fire.* What things are testing your faith right now? What struggles have you encountered in the past? Identify difficult trials your teammates and coaches might be going through. Brainstorm specific ways you can walk with and encourage each other to stand strong.

My GamePlan

_____

_____

_____

_____

_____

_____

Father, I know that storms are not optional, but inevitable. And I know that You use trials to transform me and change me into the person You have designed me to be. Let me rejoice when I face trials and struggles and trust that You have a reason. Form my character through the fire. Make me look more like Jesus. Let me face each trial with expanding faith. Let me bring You glory as I tell of Your faithfulness. And let me encourage others in their struggle as well. Amen.

22

THE CHALLENGE FLAG

WisdomWalks Principle
Review your life film.

We occasionally stumble over the truth,
but most of us pick ourselves up and hurry off as if nothing happened.
WINSTON CHURCHILL

I love the coach's challenge flag in football. Sometimes we'll rewind the action and take a closer look before they even show an instant replay. And we yell at the TV screen for the coach to throw the red flag before they can get off their next snap of the football. We can't wait for the ref to say the famous words, "After further review..." Instant replay is a game changer! Touchdowns have been reversed, home runs put on the board, turnovers taken away, catches confirmed—you name it.

The challenge flag puts the power in the hands of the coach. If the coach throws the flag, the referees have to review the film and make sure they got the call right. They are forced to face the replay and the call they made. But it also gives them a chance to get it right. Making the right call "after further review" often affects the outcome of the game and potentially the success of the season.

In sports, we have the luxury of pressing PAUSE, rewinding, and closely scrutinizing each play in slow motion and from multiple angles. But in life, we don't. Can you imagine if we had instant replay for our lives? What if we had the ability to immediately review decisions we made or things we said or did? Then, based on what we saw, we could make the right decision. Personally, I can think of things I said or did that I'd love a "do-over" on—they could make a big difference in my life!

God gives each of us challenge flags. These flags aren't for us to throw at others—unless we're given permission. Instead, He asks us to give them to our inner circle of friends, trusting that they will throw the flag to challenge our attitudes and our actions when necessary. We call this inner circle of friends *Warriors*—the people we trust to hold us accountable to the goal of becoming everything God designed us to be. We give them an all-access pass to challenge certain areas of our lives.

If you've been trusted with a challenge flag, it's your responsibility to throw it when needed—to challenge your Warriors to walk as Jesus did in every area of their lives. In 2 Samuel 12, the Lord sent Nathan to David. Nathan told David a hypothetical story very similar to what David had sinfully done with Bathsheba that resulted in the death of her husband, Uriah. After David heard the story:

> *[He] burned with anger against the man and said to Nathan, "As surely as the* LORD *lives, the man who did this deserves to die! He must pay four times over, because he did such a thing and had no pity."*
>
> *Then Nathan said to David, "You are the man!"*
>
> 2 SAMUEL 12:5–7

The challenge flag was thrown. The film was reviewed. And David was confronted with his own sin. It broke him, and he returned to God in confession and repentance. It restored his soul.

I believe God wants each of us to review the film. A sports performance coach will often videotape athletes doing specific movements, point out mistakes, and correct them. And coaches regularly review practice and game film to evaluate performance and make improvements. Studying game film is common. But studying life film is rare. With our busyness and utter lack of quiet connection to God in prayer, we rarely review life film. But David learned how important it is:

> *Search me, O God, and know my heart; test me and know my anxious thoughts. See if there is any offensive way in me, and lead me in the way everlasting.*
>
> PSALM 139:23–24

When we allow God to look at the deepest areas of our hearts from different angles and in slow motion and then say, "After further review...," we are confronted with the reality of our words, our attitudes, and our behavior. God gives us, like He did with David, an opportunity to come clean, to confess, and to repent. First John 1:9 says, "If we confess our sins, he is faithful and just and will forgive us our sins and purify us from all unrighteousness." In Acts 3:19 we are encouraged, "Repent, then, and turn to God, so that your sins may be wiped out, that times of refreshing may come from the Lord." That is God's goal: to get us to turn our hearts back to Him, to relieve us of the burden of sin, and to refresh us so we can make a difference.

So review your life film daily, asking God to reveal what needs to change. Then deal with those areas immediately. Life doesn't come with "do-overs," but coming clean restores your connection with God and grows your faith.

And allowing your Warriors carte blanche to throw challenge flags in your life will help you become the man or woman you are meant to be. Review your life film. What needs to change?

Be a GameChanger!

Live Intentionally. Maximize Relationships. Pass the Torch.

Live It

Have you ever given a close friend permission to throw the challenge flag? Did it help you to see and do something differently? If so, how?

Have you ever asked God to review your life film with you? How might this be a valuable way to end each day?

Maximize It

Read 2 Samuel 11 and 12; Proverbs 27:17. How important is it to have a Warrior like Nathan to confront you?

Ask God to examine your life film today. Ask Him to reveal things that need to change.

Pass It

Grab a teammate and discuss the *WisdomWalks* principle: *Review your life film.* In what areas of life do you want or need to be challenged? Brainstorm ways you and other leaders on the team can create a culture of accountability.

My GamePlan

_____

_____

_____

_____

_____

_____

_____

_____

_____

_____

_____

_____

_____

Father, I confess that I don't spend enough time letting You examine my heart and actions. I have a desire to walk in integrity. Help me find fellow Warriors I can trust with a challenge flag so they can help me get it right in life. Expose my sin and make me into the likeness of Christ. Amen.

23

PRIDE BOMBS

WisdomWalks Principle
Speak life, not death.

Let another praise you, and not your own mouth;
someone else, and not your own lips.
PROVERBS 27:2

I did it again. I can't believe I haven't learned yet. I should know better, but it's so hard not to do it. Everyone does it. I guess it's just considered part of life, but I refuse to cave in and be like everyone else.

While I was talking on the phone the other day with one of my accountability partners, I got fired up because we were having an awesome conversation. For some strange reason, I felt the need to slip in a quick, small, innocent sentence. Or so I thought. We were discussing the response we received from a fellow FCA staff member, and I quickly inserted, "Yeah, and he is a GOOD friend of mine." I wanted to make sure my accountability partner knew of my significant relationship with this staff member. I wasn't letting him know that I was friends with him; I was implying that things worked out because of my tight relationship with him. I was making myself look good, bragging. But it was destructive, like dropping a pride bomb!

As soon as I said it, my accountability partner responded, 'Why did you have to say that?"

I didn't respond.

He then said, "Dan, if you need encouragement, just let me know, and I will give it to you." Ouch. His accountability stung. But he was absolutely right! Not only was I praising myself, I was also fishing for praise. I wanted him to think better of me. My small, "innocent" comment screamed, "Look at me! I'm important! I'm significant!" T. S. Eliot was right when he wrote, "Most of the trouble in the world is caused by people wanting to be important." Not only did my comment turn the spotlight on me, but it also removed God from the situation. I'd blown up a great, God-centered conversation with a pride bomb.

Pride bombs are unnecessary statements we make that puff ourselves up. Others can hear them go off a mile away, and they produce the most awful, selfish odor. They reek of self-glorification. In the world of sports, unfortunately, they have become a natural part of the language. Athletes and coaches often aren't even aware that they do it, and, even if they are, they brag about it.

Why do we have such a need to brag? Do we really want people to think we have a big head or are on an ego trip? Do we want to be tagged as cocky, full of ourselves, and puffed up? Why is it so hard for us to recognize it in ourselves when others can spot it a mile away? Do we feel that we need to prove something to someone? Will others like us more if they know how important we are? Is there something missing in our lives that we want others to fill?

Maybe the reason is answered by the Spanish proverb, "Tell me what you brag about, and I'll tell you what you lack." What's really crazy is that while we do this so that others will like us more, it only makes them want to avoid us. That is messed up.

No foul language is to come from your mouth, but only what is good for building up someone in need, so that it gives grace to those who hear.

EPHESIANS 4:29 (HCSB)

As Christians, God has called us to a higher standard. He does not want us to go with the flow. He wants us to be humble and to speak with words of grace and thankfulness. Our conversations should puff others up. We should look for opportunities to slip in encouragement. I think it's safe to say that God wants us to drop encouragement bombs instead of pride bombs. The two bombs are much alike, with the exception of one small distinction: the replacement of the word *I* with the word *you. Encouragement bombs say, "You are great." Pride bombs say, "I am great."* It's that simple.

Instead of letting our comments drip with self-exhortation, we should drench them in the edification and blessing of others. I can name several people in my life that I actively seek out because of the encouragement they offer. They are gifted to build others up with authentic, genuine encouragement bombs. When they go off, the effect is love, joy, compassion, blessing, and motivation.

If we are truly walking in accordance with the will of God, we will drop encouragement bombs everywhere we go, and He will use them to bring healing and restoration to your team, your school, your family, and even your community! May we all be committed to bringing change to our teams, homes, schools, or offices through priceless bombs of encouragement. I firmly believe that everyone is under-encouraged, so there is a lot of work to be done. Today, will you speak life, or death? The choice is yours.

Be a GameChanger!

Live Intentionally. Maximize Relationships. Pass the Torch.

Live It

Reflect on your conversations over the past week on the field of competition, at home, with your friends. When did you drop encouragement bombs?

When did you drop pride bombs? Why did you feel the need to do that?

Read Proverbs 25:27; 2 Corinthians 10:12; 12:11. What do these verses say about pride and the effects of pride?

Maximize It

Of the athletes or coaches you know, who drops the best encouragement bombs? What makes this competitor different? How does this person affect the team?

How do pride bombs influence your team members and coaches? What kind of culture results on the team as a result?

As a competitor, how can encouragement become a part of everything you do?

Pass It

Grab a teammate and discuss the *WisdomWalks* principle: *Speak life, not death.* When are each of you most tempted to drop pride bombs? How can you instead turn those into encouragement bombs? Brainstorm different ways you could encourage others on your team.

My GamePlan

_____

_____

_____

_____

_____

_____

_____

_____

_____

Lord, please forgive me for dropping pride bombs. They do not honor You or others. I know You want me to speak blessings, encouragement, and love. Today, I have the opportunity to unleash favor upon others. As a competitor for Christ, I desire for You to free up my tongue and unlock my heart. Let it flow so that athletes and coaches can be touched and impacted. In the name of Jesus, I pray, amen.

24

NO EXCUSES

WisdomWalks Principle
Excuses lead to failure.

*Ninety-nine percent of failures come from people
who have the habit of making excuses.*
GEORGE WASHINGTON CARVER

When I was twelve, I was playing second base for an all-star team in an area-wide tournament. Our team was good, and we had a legitimate shot to win it all. I can still remember the smell of the grass and the light rain that started to fall in the late innings. And I still remember dropping that routine pop-up that ended up, in part, costing us the win. I went from hero to heel. So I did what most athletes do—I made excuses. I blamed the rain and lights (it was a night game). I figured my teammates blamed me, so I blamed the three guys who couldn't get hits to score runners in scoring position in the bottom of the ninth. At the time, I didn't think I was making excuses. I just didn't want the loss to be my fault.

Making excuses is the ultimate blame game. Excuses spread like a virus and make the entire team sick. That's because we win as a team and lose as a team—with everyone playing a part.

Gatorade recently reintroduced one of its popular sports drinks under the label NO EXCUSES. It's meant to be an ongoing motivational message. But in a culture that likes to come up with all the reasons things don't work out, it's not only a refreshing drink but a refreshing return to personal responsibility.

We make excuses for everything—for why we're late to practice, why we gained weight, why we didn't work out, why we missed a shot, why we did poorly on a test, you name it. We point the finger at everybody else and fail to take responsibility for the part we played.

I love this quote by Don Wilder: "Excuses are the nails used to build a house of failure." It implies that every excuse we make may seem insignificant, but in the end it helps hold together a life of failure. Excuses build the house, and then we move in and get comfortable there. Excuses allow us to lower the bar. They prevent us from striving for excellence. When we justify why we didn't do what we said we would do, it's easier to make excuses the next time. If we can't explain why we're in a particular situation, then we point the finger.

In John 5, Jesus finds a man who had been crippled for thirty-eight years. "He asked him, 'Do you want to get well?' 'Sir,' the invalid replied, 'I have no one to help me into the pool when the water is stirred. While I am trying to get in, someone else goes down ahead of me'" (John 5:6–7).

I find it amazing that the man didn't even answer Jesus' question. He immediately offered excuses. A simpler answer would have been, "Yes, I want to be healed!"

We all make excuses for ball games and even for why we don't believe. In Luke 14, Jesus exposes excuses again and tells us thatthose who don't believe will make up many excuses. Those who had been invited to the Great Banquet feast found many excuses for not attending, but none of the reasons were genuine. "But they all alike began to make excuses. The first said, 'I have just bought a field, and I must go and see it. Please excuse me.' Another said, 'I have just bought five yoke of oxen, and I'm on my way to try them out. Please excuse me.' Still another said, 'I just got married, so I can't come'" (Luke 14:18–20).

Excuses never make you better. And they don't change your circumstances—they solidify them. When making excuses becomes a habit, we're running on a road to failure. These three words are a sure sign that what comes next is an excuse: *could've, would've*, and *should've*. "I could've started on the varsity, but (*insert excuse here*)." "I would've fielded that pop-up, but (*insert excuse here*)." "I should've won that race, but (*insert excuse here*)." It's always the same.

The only antidote for excuses is to take *and* make. Take full responsibility and make changes. We have a choice to either *deflect* or *accept* responsibility. One of the ten guiding principles at my kids' school is "Take full responsibility for your actions and their consequences." They probably could have shortened it to "No excuses." When we take responsibility, we exercise a spirit of humility and consider others as better than ourselves. We assume ownership of both the problem and the solution.

A wise person once said, "Those who are good at making excuses are seldom good at anything else." So don't get good at making excuses. Excuses lead to failure. If it's important enough, you'll find a way. If not, you'll find an excuse. Instead, take responsibility and make changes!

⟨ Be a GameChanger! ⟩

Live Intentionally. Maximize Relationships. Pass the Torch.

Live It

Have you ever played the blame game? Why is this so destructive to your team?

Have you ever made an excuse for why things didn't go the way you had planned or committed to? When—and why?

Maximize It

Think about what you say in the locker room after a tough loss. Do you take personal responsibility, or do you tend to make excuses? Do you deflect or accept the blame? Why?

What kind of excuses do you hear in the locker room from other teammates? How do the coaches respond? How do your athletes respond?

Read Luke 18:9–14; Philippians 2:2–4. Why is it easier to blame someone else or think of ourselves as better than others? From these passages, what is the key to taking responsibility? Why do you think the tax collector left a changed man?

Read Luke 6:41–42; Romans 12:3. How would believing in the power of these verses affect the culture of your team? Would you be more or less likely to take full responsibility? Why?

Pass It

Grab a teammate and discuss the *WisdomWalks* principle: *Excuses lead to failure.* Hold each other accountable to listen to your words carefully this week. Do you make excuses? Or take responsibility and make changes? Lead by example—personally take ownership of the problems and responsibility for the solutions. Find ways to encourage coaches and teammates to do the same.

My GamePlan

\
\
\
\
\
\
\
\

Father, show me ways that I've become an excuse maker. Reveal to me how I've blamed others when things didn't go as planned. Help me really listen to the words I speak. I know excuses lead to failure, and I don't want to be on that road. Remind me to take personal responsibility and to make the changes necessary for excellence. Amen.

25

KING OF THE HILL

WisdomWalks Principle
Depend on Him to shut down sin.

Our scientific power has outrun our spiritual power.
We have guided missiles and misguided men.
MARTIN LUTHER KING JR.

In the game of baseball, Mariano Rivera of the New York Yankees is the King of the Hill. He recently became the sport's all-time greatest closer with over six hundred saves. As a Yankee fan, if I saw Mariano coming out of the bullpen, I knew the game was over. In fact, I knew that if we had a lead going into the ninth inning, it was lights out for the other team. And, if they were honest, his opponents would admit the same thing. He was virtually unhittable. He saw the bat as his enemy and broke many of them with his devastating "cutter" fastball.

Power means having control, authority, or influence. In sports, *power = strength in motion.* Mariano was a picture of power from the pitcher's mound. He shut down his opponent game after game. But he realized that his power to pitch was a gift. When others suggest his success was a combination of a powerful right arm, consistent work ethic, and a fighter's will, he laughs. And while he admits you have to have talent to play in the big leagues, he says his talent wasn't enough; he credits God. When he was in the minor leagues, he was throwing an average 88 mph. Then it jumped to 95–98 mph. He says, "Who can explain that?" Mariano believes it was the power of God.

We often trust in our own power or ability instead of God's. We like to take credit. We like to think we are in control. Ironically, even the ability we think we've worked so hard to get is really a gift from the One who created us. Psalm 20:7 says, "Some trust in chariots and some in horses, but we trust in the name of the LORD our God."

We all want power for living. Having the power to perform well in sports is one thing. Having power for life is something else entirely. Winston Churchill once said, "The power of man has grown in every sphere, except over himself." Even with our best efforts, if we are to live a life of power, we need a power greater than ourselves.

In life we have three opponents—the lies of the Devil, the lure of our flesh, and the love of the world. Jesus has given us power over all three.

> *Do not love this world nor the things it offers you, for when you love the world, you do not have the love of the Father in you. For the world offers only a craving for physical pleasure, a craving for everything we see, and pride in our achievements and possessions. These are not from the Father, but are from this world.*

1 John 2:15-16 NLT

We have power over our flesh. We all face temptations and peer pressure. We all are tempted to give in to the "craving for physical pleasure." Whether it's a sexual temptation, a desire for alcohol or drugs, excessive food, or even laziness, our flesh wants what it wants when it wants it. But Paul tells us, "The temptations in your life are no different from what others experience. And God is faithful. He will not allow the temptation to be more than you can stand. When you are tempted, he will show you a way out so that you can endure" (1 Corinthians 10:13 NLT).

We often think we're strong enough to "do it on our own." But we need the power of God. He gives us the strength to stand or flee. He always gives us a way out!

We have power over the world. The Enemy loves to appeal to our sense of pride in what we've done and what we have. We brag about our victories and take credit when things go right; we even believe we're the King of the Hill. Sometimes we act humble, but we swell up on the inside. Then the Enemy shows us all the attractions this world has to offer. Whether it's the latest iPhone, a pair of designer jeans, a car—material things never satisfy for long. The Bible tells us, though, that "His divine power has given us everything we need for life and godliness...so...[we] may participate in the divine nature and escape the corruption of the world caused by evil desires" (2 Peter 1:3–4).

The Enemy appeals to our desire for all these things, knowing they will end up crowding out our love for the Father. But we can have victory.

We have power over the Devil. Our Enemy is not to be taken lightly. His singular purpose is to destroy us: "Your enemy the devil prowls around like a roaring lion looking for someone to devour" (1 Peter 5:8). He tries to deceive us and distract us from obeying God. He appeals to our cravings and tempts us, but God has given us power to stand. James 4:7 (NLT) says, "So humble yourselves before God. Resist the devil and he will flee from you."

We must walk in the Spirit and see the attempts of the Enemy to derail us. Our strength is not enough. We need the power of the Holy Spirit living in us to overcome our sin.

God is the ultimate King of the Hill, and the Holy Spirit lives in you. In order to live a life of power, we must depend on Him to shut down sin.

Be a GameChanger!

Live Intentionally. Maximize Relationships. Pass the Torch.

Live It

Read Colossians 3:1–5. Do you experience power over the desires of your flesh? Or do you easily give in to temptation? Explain.

What does it mean to set your heart and mind on things above?

How can we put to death whatever belongs to our earthly nature?

Maximize It

Read 2 Corinthians 10:4. What are the weapons we use to fight with power?

How can you incorporate these weapons into your daily routine?

Read Acts 1:8; 2 Corinthians 12:9; 2 Timothy 1:7. What do these verses say about how God's power works in you?

If you could do one thing for maximum spiritual growth and life change, what would it be?

Pass It

Grab a teammate and discuss the *WisdomWalks* principle: *Depend on Him to shut down sin.* In what life areas are each of you most vulnerable to the traps of the Enemy? Find ways to encourage coaches and teammates to overcome the temptations they face by relying on God's power.

My GamePlan

_____

_____

_____

_____

_____

_____

_____

_____

Father, I desire to have the power to overcome the lies of the Devil, the lure of my flesh, and the love of the things of this world. I need the power of the Holy Spirit to fill me so I can resist temptation. Help me set my heart and mind on things above so I don't fall for the traps here below. Help me to depend on You and shut down sin. Amen.

26

RISKY PRAYER

WisdomWalks Principle
Prayer unleashes God's power.

There is nothing too hard for God to do.
God has pledged if we ask, we shall receive.
God can withhold nothing from faith and prayer.

E. M. BOUNDS

The atmosphere was filled with tension. Players from both teams had been encouraged to protest the game. An outside source was trying to convince players they were being exploited by big-time college sports. Everyone was anticipating a conflict, but what people didn't expect, including the seventy-four thousand fans watching, was some risky prayer!

This 1986 historic football game became one of the greatest between No. 3 Oklahoma and No. 5 Nebraska. Oklahoma's running back Spencer Tillman and Nebraska's Stan Parker decided to do the unthinkable. They led several of their teammates to midfield prior to the opening kickoff. The crowd watched in awe as they knelt down, holding hands at the 50-yard line in Lincoln, Nebraska. It was risky prayer. People wanted them to protest, but they prayed. It wasn't the statement people were expecting. The act of kneeling was not a prideful statement to impress people; rather it was a humble act to show people who they played for. *They had a higher calling— they played for the Audience of One.* This simple act of prayer and courage let people know that they were only controlled by the One who created them.

They prayed the game would be a clean, hard-fought, injury-free contest to honor God Himself. It was a commitment to excellence for all to see. There was no protest other than to say, "We protest everything not wholesome or fair. We protest failure, disrespect, and those ungrateful for moments like this." They prayed according to Matthew 18:20: "For where two or three come together in my name, there am I with them." They put God on display. It was risky.

We now see prayer after games all the time. It has almost become tradition. But when is the last time you saw pre-game prayer at the center of the field or court? Players coming together as competitors, not enemies, who desire to help one another play their best? It would be a way of showing everyone that God comes first, not last. How many times have you ended something like an activity, task, project, or game, and said, "Okay, now let's ask God to bless this"? Instead, we should say, "Before we even start, let's pray and ask God to be at the center of everything we do."

Risky prayer is when you start with prayer, not end with prayer. It is praying instead of protesting. Bending a knee, not raising a fist. It is joining with the competition in prayer before sweating.

That game turned out to be unbelievable. After tying the score at 17 with 1:22 left, Oklahoma got the ball back in the dying seconds. Facing a fourth-and-12, Oklahoma's Keith Jackson made a one-handed catch at the Nebraska 14. Oklahoma kicked the winning 31-yard field goal at 0:06. The score ended with Oklahoma—20, Nebraska—17.

Even though seventy-four thousand fans were challenged by that powerful act of risky prayer, the biggest blessing was for those nine players. When we are obedient and respond to the Lord's prompting, we grow, change, and become transformed. Those players tapped into a powerful spiritual principle, "Prayer unleashes God's power." It changes us, and it changes the way we look at circumstances. Changing us is even more miraculous than changing the situation.

I want men everywhere to lift up holy hands in prayer, without anger or disputing.

1 TIMOTHY 2:8

Prayer has a way of putting things into perspective. It resets the heart, makes things clear, and eliminates the noise. Prayer can be risky because of where we pray. When it is done in public, we have to check our hearts and make sure we are not doing it for personal gain or attention. The religious leaders in the Bible were notorious for praying in public so everyone could see how spiritual they were. And Jesus let them have it for their prideful prayer. Risky prayer is when God gets the glory; prideful prayer is when we get the glory. Risky prayer is not only where we pray, but *what* we pray. How might the world change if we all prayed as if we believed our prayers—even the risky ones—would be answered?

Risky prayer also involves courage. It pushes us out of our comfort zone. Courage is simply doing what we know is right, even when it is hard. Instead of protesting our competition, we pray with them. Instead of criticizing, we pray. Instead of disputing, we pray.

God has called you, competitor, to be willing to engage in risky prayer. Those prayers will change you and your team and spread far beyond. But be ready—because when you pray such a prayer, God is bound to show up powerfully. He loves risky prayer.

Be a GameChanger!

Live Intentionally. Maximize Relationships. Pass the Torch.

Live It

Why was it risky for the Oklahoma and Nebraska players to pray before the game? Would you have done it? Have you witnessed an example of risky prayer? What makes it risky?

Do you pray first—before things begin on the field—or after? What is the value of each?

Read 1 Kings 18:16–46; Psalm 50:15; Luke 11:1–4; Colossians 1:9–12. What do these verses say about risky prayer? In what way(s) do they influence your desire to connect to God through prayer?

Maximize It

Why does risky prayer require humility and courage? If you've prayed a risky prayer, what was the result?

In 1 Kings 18:16–46, Elijah engaged in risky prayer. Why was his prayer so risky? What did he have to lose?

How can risky prayer become a part of everything you do?

Pass It

Grab a teammate and discuss the *WisdomWalks* principle: *Prayer unleashes God's power.* Brainstorm some different ways you and your teammate could encourage each other to pray risky prayers. How might your team set aside time to pray together with courage and boldness?

My GamePlan

_____

_____

_____

_____

_____

_____

_____

_____

_____

Almighty God in heaven, help me to have a pure heart when I pray. I do not want to pray to get attention. All glory goes to You, Lord. Open my eyes to opportunities for risky prayer. I ask for wisdom to know when to pray, even when it takes me out of my comfort zone. Thank You for allowing me to call upon You, the God of the universe, for help. Amen.

27

BE AN IRONMAN

WisdomWalks Principle
Manage your energy for the winning edge.

Pain is weakness leaving the body.
US MARINE CORPS

I love to compete in triathlons. Each discipline—swim, bike, run—has unique challenges. In my first triathlon, I remember thinking I could drown. As an experienced swimmer, this was totally unexpected. But as competitors battled for position in the water, I was kicked, hit, and pulled on. I still have the vision of someone going right over the top of me in the water. I did my fair share of praying that day for sure.

But I've never attempted the Ironman distance. The Ironman Triathlon is considered the toughest one-day sporting event in the world—a test of the mind, the body, and the soul. The race starts early with a 2.4-mile swim, transitions to 112 miles on the bike, then finishes with a full 26.2 mile marathon! The fastest professionals finish the race in under eight hours; some mere mortals finish in fourteen hours, crossing the finish line well after the sun has set; still others fail to finish. You could easily argue that the three-sport triathlete is the ultimate endurance athlete.

The sport of triathlon is a great picture of what it takes for peak performance in sport and in life. We need to manage our energy in three dimensions—mind, body, and spirit. Weakness in any single dimension affects the others and diminishes our overall potential and performance. We are only as strong as our weakest link.

Each of us has things that either fill us with energy or drain us. Some people think all stress is bad and that our goal should be to eliminate it. Others thrive under pressure and think every aspect of life should be fueled by the adrenaline caused by stress. Both extremes are dangerous. Being over-stressed leads to burnout and breakdown; being under-stressed leads to atrophy and weakness. The better we know how to fill our energy tanks and plug the energy drains, the better we perform.

The Mind. In the Bible, the mind is often referred to as our thoughts, will, and emotions. Negative thinking leads to destructive emotions that result in poor choices—thus draining our mental and emotional energy. If we want to be different, we have to change the way we think.

Winners are intentionally optimistic. They reject negativity, even in the midst of tremendous challenges or adversity. Winners will not accept discouragement or defeat. They always believe it will get better, and they take responsibility for their role. A coach once told our team on the sideline when we trailed by ten points, "We've got 'em right where we want 'em." That's intentional optimism. We all began to believe.

Winners make decisions in advance. They know they can't train just when they feel like it. Doing the little things each day requires mental toughness and disciplined thinking. Everything is a choice.

Winners guard their thoughts. They "take in the truth" of God's Word, thinking about what is possible, pure, right, and noble (Philippians 4:8), and "take out the trash" of criticism, negativity, doubt, and defeat.

Winners remove clutter. Distractions—such as the constant multitasking noise of texting, web searches, Facebook, iPods—divert our focus and deplete our energy to respond to pressure situations. Even living in a cluttered room can drain mental energy and hurt performance.

The Body. Athletes know how to push their physical bodies beyond normal limits, but some push so hard they get injured; others never take a break and end up quitting the sport altogether. When we push too hard without recovery and rest, we're going to hit the wall. Physical tiredness affects our thoughts and emotions, and we make more mistakes. Vince Lombardi once said, "Fatigue makes cowards of us all." Rested, well-fueled athletes perform at their best. The food we eat fuels our energy levels and helps give our bodies what they need to recover and grow. We're able to maintain focus and concentration, have better speed and strength, and respond much better to adversity.

The Spirit. Our relationship with God fills us with an inner sense of identity, security, and purpose. It fuels the "why," giving us a bigger purpose and the energy we need (1 Peter 4:11). And when the why is big enough, it drives the "what" and the "how." Why are you competing? Why are you training? *Great athletes always have a huge why.* And the why can never be just about yourself. In Galatians 1:10, Paul says, "Am I now trying to win the approval of human beings, or of God? Or am I trying to please people? If I were still trying to please people, I would not be a servant of Christ."

Winners are connected to God daily and filled with the Spirit; they are not drained by a need to please others. *They play to please God,* knowing their value as a person does not depend on their performance. When who you are depends on how you perform, your worth is always tied to your last game, creating tremendous pressure that drains your joy and love for the game.

Our energy tanks are constantly being filled or drained. As competitors, we need to manage our energy for peak performance. Dr. Jarrod Spencer, a good friend of mine and top sports psychologist, says it best: "It doesn't matter how much 'natural talent' a competitor has; if their energy is low—mind, body, and spirit—their capacity to handle stress is drained and performance will suffer." A clearer mind results in better performance. A tested and rested body does, too. And when our spiritual energy tank is full of God's presence, we are able to take on the world. Manage your energy for the winning edge.

Be a GameChanger!

Live Intentionally. Maximize Relationships. Pass the Torch.

Live It

What fills or drains your mental and emotional energy?

What fills or drains your physical energy?

What fills or drains your spiritual energy?

Maximize It

Read Romans 8:5; 2 Corinthians 10:5; Philippians 4:8. What are ways you can mentally remove clutter and "take in the truth" and "take out the trash"?

Read Colossians 3:23–24; 1 Thessalonians 2:4; 1 Peter 4:11. What is your spiritual "why" for competing? Is it a big enough "why" to keep you going when things get tough?

Pass It

Grab a teammate and discuss the *WisdomWalks* principle: *Manage your energy for the winning edge.* How can you fill each other's energy tanks? Identify the things that drain your energy as a team. Get a plan together to increase the total energy of your team—mind, body, and spirit.

My GamePlan

_____

_____

_____

_____

_____

_____

_____

_____

_____

Father, thank You for making me a three-dimensional athlete. Help me identify the things in my life that drain my energy and cause stress. Change the way I think; change the way I fuel my body and find rest; change the way I connect with You. Fill me with Your supernatural energy that I need to live and compete at my best! Amen.

28

POSTING UP

WisdomWalks Principle
God loves spiritual sweat.

God, You are my God; I eagerly seek You. I thirst for You;
my body faints for You in a land that is dry, desolate, and without water.
PSALM 63:1 HCSB

The NBA Finals are the best. You can skip watching NBA all year, but you have to tune in once the playoffs start. The key matchups these games bring are intriguing—for example, the Lakers and Celtics competing against each other for the title for the twelfth time, and the key player matchups, such as Rondo/Bryant and Pierce/Artest.

Even though lacrosse was my primary sport, I loved to play basketball as a kid. I invested hours in front of the driveway hoop over our garage. At six foot one, I didn't have much height for a forward, so I quickly learned the art and importance of posting up against the defense.

I found a great description on www.coachesclipboard.net about what it means to post up:

Posting up is to establish a position in the low post, the area near the basket below the foul line, usually in order to take advantage of a smaller defender. As the offensive player, you usually face away from the basket, so that your body can protect the ball from the defender. You set a wide, stable stance, which gives you more power. Usually you can use your outside hand to get the ball, while your inside hand can fend off the defense and keep control. You call for the ball. From this position, options such as spinning or backing down the defender to close in to the basket for better scoring opportunities become available to you.

At times, when you see big men posting up, it appears to be an all-out battle. Those guys are doing whatever it takes to get position and get the ball. Even though I don't post up on the court like I used to, I do a different type of posting up every day. It's a battle, and it's for positioning, but it's not about basketball. This kind of posting up involves the Lord and me.

Every morning, I post up to get the Word of God in me. Since I joined His team, I need to be ready, prepared. I have to post up. Take a second right now to reread that official description of posting up but in spiritual terms. It's a great analogy, doesn't it?

In 1 Timothy 4:7–8, Paul says physical training has some value, *but spiritual training has double value—for this life and the life to come.* When we work out with God, spiritual sweat is created, and we change. A transformation takes place when we engage God. Our spirit grows and becomes strong. We are preparing ourselves to be in shape spiritually for the game of life.

> *God, You are my God; I eagerly seek You.*
> *I thirst for You;*
> *my body faints for You*
> *in a land that is dry, desolate, and without water.*
>
> PSALM 63:1 HCSB

When it comes to the spiritual post up, I've learned three helpful tips to living with purpose and intentionality.

1. *Establish position.* Many people have never gained position over the competition—the flesh, the Devil, and the world. We need to face away from the competition and live a separated life (Romans 12:1–2). We must have a strong stance and not be rocked by this world. We need to stand strong against the opponent. It's a daily battle.

2. *Call for the ball.* You don't post up for the fun of it, but to get the ball. Are you calling out to the Lord and asking Him to show up and speak to you? To reveal to you the deeper things? He desires to pass His Word to you daily, but you need to ask for it.

3. *Make a play and score.* Once you get the ball, you are in the position to make an impact. Each day, when you fill up with God's Word, you are ready to serve, minister, love, and invest in others.

The Lord is ready to pass you the ball. He wants to bless you each day as you post up. Our competition is tough, and many things get position on us and try to prevent us from posting up. It's an all-out war for our souls, and whatever the opponent needs to do to distract you, he will do it. Maybe you need to post up right now and call upon the Lord. Know that He is waiting for you.

Make space for Him to speak to you. Practice the discipline of posting up. Understand the power it brings. Remember, the Lord loves to see His players establishing position, calling for the ball, and making a play.

Be a GameChanger!

Live Intentionally. Maximize Relationships. Pass the Torch.

Live It

What is the hardest part about posting up physically? As an athlete, what prevents us from posting up?

What is the hardest part of posting up spiritually? List at least three specific things that distract you from posting up.

When do you post up? Is that the best time for you for maximum impact? Why or why not? What might work better?

Maximize It

What would it mean for you to make a play spiritually—using the gifts and talents God has given you—and score?

Read Deuteronomy 4:29; 1 Chronicles 28:9; 2 Chronicles 7:14; Psalm 34:10, 84:2; Matthew 6:33. Why does God long for you to post up daily? What is the benefit to both you and Him? What is the benefit to your teammates?

How might posting up daily influence your relationships in all arenas? How might it impact you as a competitor?

Pass It

Grab a teammate and discuss the *WisdomWalks* principle: *God loves spiritual sweat.* Talk about how posting up—or not—impacts your personal life and your work on the field. Brainstorm specific ways you can encourage each other to post up daily. Then see how it impacts your plays as a team!

My GamePlan

_____

_____

_____

_____

_____

_____

_____

_____

_____

_____

_____

Lord, I want to understand Your heart and Your plan for my life. Things can easily crowd out the time and get in the way of my ability to create space for You to show up. Teach me the discipline of posting up. Help me daily to box out the competition. Nothing is more important than connecting with You. I commit to posting up daily, starting today. In the name of Jesus, I pray, amen.

29

CALL TIME-OUT

WisdomWalks Principle
Rest brings refreshment.

Come with me by yourselves to a quiet place and get some rest.
JESUS, IN MARK 6:31

Have you ever been part of a game that seems out of control? Your opponent scores several points in a row and gets all the breaks. And no matter what adjustments you make, nothing helps. You need to do something—*anything*—to change things before the game is lost. That's when everybody on your team and even the spectators in the stands stand up together and yell, "Call time-out!"

I've been there. In fact, there are many ways to get to a point in a game and in life where we need to call a time-out. Sometimes we're overwhelmed by everything we need to get done. Other times we over-coach, over-train, or even push through injuries. We're afraid to take time off because we think we might get behind. In the process, we get worn out. Some of us push so hard that we should call back-to-back time-outs.

Rest brings refreshment. The more we know about the effects of proper rest, the more we marvel at God's perfect design. When He created the world, He incorporated *a rhythm of rest for both our daily and weekly routines.* Each day God gives us light and dark, and He planted in us an internal clock to regulate our wake/sleep cycle. And each week He set aside a day specifically for us to rest.

It turns out that God knew we needed regular rest in order to be at our best. He designed us that way. But our frantic schedules and busyness tear us down. And the noise from all our technology prevents us from unplugging at all. But God has given us two primary gifts to ensure that we can unplug and escape. If we follow His plan, we will be regularly refreshed and renewed in mind, body, and soul.

The first gift is the Sabbath. In Genesis 2:2, God set an example for us by resting from all of His creative work. He then commanded us to do the same. The writer of Hebrews drove the point home in chapter 4, verses 9–10 (HCSB):

A Sabbath rest remains, therefore, for God's people. For the person who has entered His rest has rested from his own works, just as God did from His.

The Sabbath is a once-a-week opportunity for God to breathe life back into our weary souls. He wants us to set our minds and hearts on Him so He can reset our priorities and revitalize us. He even lets us pick the day and gives us freedom how to spend it. But make no mistake: He wants us to rest. It's a gift for us to receive and enjoy.

By taking one day to rest, we realize He is in control, that we need Him, and that we depend on His provision. Unfortunately, many of us refuse to take a day each week. We simply have too much to do. We find it hard to trust that we can get everything done that God designed us to get done in only six days.

In our 24/7 culture, finding a regular Sabbath is almost unheard of, but God knows we will be at our best when we receive this gift and protect a day.

The second gift is sleep. If you want to perform better on the field—and in life—sleep might just be your secret weapon. A study conducted by sleep expert Dr. Bill Dement from Stanford University evaluated eleven players from the university's men's basketball team. For the study, the athletes were asked to increase their sleep to ten hours per night. What a dream come true for a college student! While most of the athletes still slept fewer than nine hours per night, the results were eye opening. Their performance improved dramatically in every area, including shooting accuracy, speed, and reaction time. Off the court, they also reported better moods and less fatigue.

Research tells us that most of us perform best and have the most energy for daily activity and athletic performance when we get between seven and nine hours of sleep each night. If we don't, we pay a heavy price in many areas of health.

Most people don't realize that lost sleep accumulates over time and creates a sleep debt. Just as we do with our money, when we spend more than we have, we go into debt. The created deficit causes stress, robs us of life, and diminishes performance.

Unless the LORD builds a house, its builders labor in vain.... In vain you get up early and stay up late, eating food earned by hard work; certainly He gives sleep to the one He loves.

PSALM 127:1–2 HCSB, ABRIDGED

We often ignore our body's natural signals that we need sleep. Instead of finding rest or getting to bed earlier, we turn to caffeine or other stimulants to help us push through. But anything other than sleep is a poor substitute for rest. Sleep is an active process that restores and rebuilds our health.

Jesus modeled how to find rest. He practiced it and taught the disciples how to find rest as well. If you want to operate at your highest level, take Him up on His offer to bless you with rest by creating a lifestyle in alignment with His Word and design. It will make all the difference on the field and in life.

So call a time-out. Rest brings refreshment.

Be a GameChanger!

Live Intentionally. Maximize Relationships. Pass the Torch.

Live It

Do you find it easy or hard to take a day of rest each week? Do you feel compelled to train so you won't fall behind? Why?

What prevents you from receiving this weekly gift of the Sabbath?

Do you get the proper amount of sleep each night needed for energized living? Are you experiencing "sleep debt"? What prevents you from enjoying this daily gift from God?

Maximize It

Read Psalm 23:2–3. When we follow God and align what we do with what His Word says, what do we receive?

Read Isaiah 40:31; Matthew 11:28–30. What does God promise if we follow His plan for rest?

Pass It

Grab a teammate and discuss the *WisdomWalks* principle: *Rest brings refreshment.* Talk about the things that prevent you from experiencing a Sabbath each week and getting the sleep you need. Brainstorm specific things you can change personally and as a team to encourage rest that honors God and improves performance. Map out your personal plan below.

My GamePlan

_____

_____

_____

_____

_____

_____

_____

Father, I confess I have not received Your gifts of the Sabbath and sleep that You designed to refresh my mind, body, and soul. Help me to discover the real reasons I can't or won't slow down. I know You desire for me to come to You to quiet my anxiety, carry my burdens, and restore my soul. Give me the strength to change my priorities, build in proper rest, and trust You with the result. Amen.

30

SHOWTIME

WisdomWalks Principle
Impress at a distance; impact up close.

Come set me free. Inside this shell there's a prison cell.
Jon Foreman, Switchfoot

I hate tennis!" Why would one of the world's best tennis players say that? Because André Agassi was trapped. In his book, *Open: An Autobiography*, Agassi said, "I play tennis for a living even though I hate tennis, hate it with a dark and secret passion and always have." As early as age seven, he wanted to quit the game he gave his life to. The unrelenting pressure from his over-bearing dad helped create a hatred for the game he played so well. Finally, at age thirty-six, he revealed the truth—he was just playing tennis for others. He was faking it the entire time.

Competing is all about performing. We prepare hard to perform well, and we quickly learn there are two outcomes: perform or perish! As competitors, we step onto the field of competition, set everything aside, and perform our best. As athletes and coaches, we have a built-in platform. We put on the jersey, look our best, and play our best—regardless of what is going on beneath the jersey. We train ourselves to not let the inside stuff—problems, conflicts, struggles—affect the outside stuff since we're still expected to compete at a high level.

We begin to think the goal is to impress the coaches, teammates, fans, parents, and friends. The pressure is to give "them" what they want—a good game, a good show. We get what we want (recognition and rewards), and they get what they want (performance and pleasure). But that's called *transactional competing*, and that type of competition traps competitors in a destructive cycle. It destroyed Agassi.

However, since the show must go on, we fake it until we make it. We master this skill on the field of competition and also apply it to everyday life. The performance mind-set in sports becomes the way we do life. And life becomes a show. *The front stage (what we present to others but not the real us) is the enemy of the soul.* We want others to see us better than who we really are. The front stage of our lives (known as our outside or false self) contradicts the back stage (known as our inside or true self). This battle rages within us daily, which creates an enormous amount of unhealthy inner tension.

Our life becomes a daily show on the main stage, with the goal to impress others. The act is rehearsed and choreographed to bring pleasure to the viewing audience. A foundational principle of the front stage is to impress at a distance but never up close.

The lie that drives us is this: the better the performance, the more they like us—and the less likely others will discover the back stage. The louder the cheers, the greater the desire to please others. Along the way, we pray that nobody will ever discover the back stage. The pain, insecurities, weaknesses, wounds, and sins in our lives are off-limits. No one is allowed behind the curtain. We hide it, bury it, and keep it in the dark where it belongs, and for sure, it must not make it to the front stage.

If the back stage is revealed, we think it will embarrass us and shock others. The front stage controls the back stage. However, deep inside we realize that as long as the front stage is in control, we will live in bondage. Jon Foreman is right when he belts out in his song "Free": "Come set me free. Inside this shell there's a prison cell." Freedom is lost for the sake of protecting the back stage. We think we are fooling others, but we are actually fooling ourselves. We think if the back stage ever becomes the front stage, it will take too much work, cause too much pain, and bring way too much regret.

Unfortunately, we believe duplicity is easier than authenticity. Performance-based living produces legalism. It destroys grace-based living. Chuck Swindoll says it well: "Being real is a lot better than looking religious. Pursuing holiness is biblical. Acting all holy stinks." Is there hope for the back stage? Is transparency possible? The cure is found in pursuing wholeness of soul and letting the love of Jesus invade our hearts. This brings healing that is desperately needed in others and us!

May God himself, the God of peace, sanctify you through and through. May your whole spirit, soul and body be kept blameless at the coming of our Lord Jesus Christ.

1 Thessalonians 5:23

The back stage and front stage must be replaced by Christ's stage. We play and live for an audience of One. No more shows. No more pretending. Sacrifice your image and restore your heart. Stop the show and get real. God does not need our performances to advance the kingdom of God. But He does need our hearts. He wants us to pursue one stage—Christ's stage. The front stage is the enemy of our souls, but Christ is the lover of our souls. And He loves us just the way we are. But He loves us too much to let us stay the way we are!

Ready. Set. Stop. Stop performing. Performance-based competition and performance-based living will kill you from the inside out. It will rob and steal your joy for competing and living. It's time to get real and be honest about your back stage. We all have one. Tear down the curtain, and let Christ reign in your life.

Be a GameChanger!

Live Intentionally. Maximize Relationships. Pass the Torch.

Live It

As competitors, why are we so good at performing in life? How does this possibly set us up for duplicity on and off the field?

How would you define your back stage? In what areas do you feel like you're pretending? Explain.

Read Romans 12:2; 2 Timothy 2:21; Titus 2:14; Hebrews 4:12. What do these verses say about the front stage and the back stage in your own life? How might they help you tear down that front stage you use to impress others?

Maximize It

Why do we think we would be embarrassed and shock others if the back stage was revealed?

Read James 4:5; 1 John 1:9. Do you have hurts, pains, wounds, or sins in your life that keep you from being honest, open, and transparent? If so, ask God to forgive them, then confess them to a trusted friend for healing and to help hold you accountable.

Pass It

Grab a teammate and discuss the *WisdomWalks* principle: *Impress at a distance; impact up close.* How can your transparency with your teammates impact them? Talk about the kind of spiritual impact each of you wants to make on your team.

My GamePlan

_____

_____

_____

_____

_____

_____

_____

Lord, I confess I have a back stage. It doesn't honor You. It's in the dark, and I know You desire for it to be in the light. My back stage can glorify You only if I am real and it becomes Your stage. I ask You to do Your work in my life on the field of competition and off the field to bring wholeness. Have Your way with me. In the name of Jesus, I pray, amen.

31

MARGIN OF VICTORY

WisdomWalks Principle
As the margin grows, victory is yours.

A wise man prefers to play with a big lead, not a big deficit.
ANONYMOUS COACH

Flash back to the closest finish in the history of swimming. Michael Phelps, in hot pursuit of an earth-shattering eight Olympic gold medals at the 2008 Beijing games, finishes his flip-turn in the 100-meter butterfly in seventh place and trailing by almost a full body length. Surely this deficit is insurmountable. Incredibly, Michael is able to close the gap, literally winning by the tip of his finger. When the times post on the giant scoreboard, everyone is stunned. Even the underwater replays seem to defy logic.

Photo finishes in sports can be thrilling! When it's impossible for the naked eye to determine the winner and the loser, we love it. Today the most sophisticated timing and video technology is available for almost every sport. In the closest finish in NASCAR racing history, Jimmie Johnson won the 2011 race at Talladega Superspeedway by .002 seconds. In the 1992 Barcelona Olympics 100-meter sprints, judges had to analyze the film to declare Gail Devers the winner. Even sports like tennis and triathlon leave nothing to chance with video replays and timing chips. When a competition is decided by a matter of inches, we get an adrenaline rush. For the winners, it's time to celebrate. For the losers, it's agonizing.

When the margin narrows, it increases the likelihood that we'll be beaten. For example, in the game of tennis, most unforced errors are caused by shots attempted with very little margin for error. And while an aggressive shot looks great when it works, risky shots are usually the difference between victory and defeat.

The same is true in life: walking the tightrope between winning and losing can have devastating effects. When margin decreases, stress increases. When margin increases, stress decreases.

The margin of victory is the difference between winning and losing. It's the difference between what we have and what we need—between our capacity and our commitments. It often seems like we go from one thing to the next, with hardly time to think. Throw in the demands of school, sports, training, work, and family, and life feels like it's pulling apart at the seams. That's called *negative* margin.

But God wants us to have *positive* margin, and that means making wise decisions.

> *Be very careful, then, how you live—not as unwise but as wise, making the most of every opportunity because the days are evil. Therefore do not be foolish, but understand what the Lord's will is.*
>
> EPHESIANS 5:15–17

We need to protect a positive margin of victory in two areas: our time and our morals.

Time margin is the difference between the time we have and the time we need. We're addicted to busy. When the alarm goes off, we hit the ground running. Unconsciously we think, *If I'm busy, I'm important. If I'm not, I'm insignificant.* But when we constantly push ourselves to the limit, it's easy to slip into the red zone of negative margin. We buy into the lie that *activity means achievement*, and we certainly don't want to fall behind. So we commit to things out of fear, have trouble saying no, and our calendar gets filled to the limit. When we have no *time margin*, just one more commitment can overwhelm us and make us feel burned out. We have to learn to say no to some good things to make time for the best things.

Moral margin is the distance between doing the right thing and doing the wrong thing. So many of us try to see how close we can get to sin without crossing the line. We keep the competition (our Enemy) in the game and even give him a shot to win! But God wants us to keep our distance from temptation. He wants us to flee from compromising situations. When we have no *moral margin*, one small mistake can bring a tidal wave of guilt, shame, and brokenness. And that brings us closer to the edge of disaster. Galatians 5:13 warns, "You, my brothers [and sisters], were called to be free. But do not use your freedom to indulge the sinful nature."

The Old Testament records the stories of Joseph and David. When Joseph found himself in a compromising situation with Potiphar's wife, he fled. But when David looked on Bathsheba's beauty, he moved closer to the line of sin and eliminated his margin of victory. His choice to cross the line left a wake of destruction behind.

When we have a narrow margin of victory with our time and morals, we are at risk for burnout or breakdown. As we increase our moral margin, we are far less likely to have a moral meltdown. As we increase our time margin, we have more energy and enthusiasm for the field and life.

As the margin grows, victory is yours.

Be a GameChanger!

Live Intentionally. Maximize Relationships. Pass the Torch.

Live It

When have you experienced the stress of a hectic schedule? How has it influenced your thoughts, feelings, and the decisions you make on a daily basis?

Read Luke 10:38–42. Have you ever been so overbooked and overwhelmed that you missed important opportunities—or were late for something important? What was the result?

Have you ever drawn the line closer and closer to what you know is sin? Do you tend to see how close you can get to temptation? Why or why not?

Maximize It

Read 1 Corinthians 10:13, 23–24. How do these verses encourage you to create moral margin to protect you from sin?

What does it mean that "everything is permissible, but not everything is beneficial"? When you encounter temptations, how can these words help you answer the question, "Is it wise?"

Pass It

Grab a teammate and discuss the *WisdomWalks* principle: *As the margin grows, victory is yours.* What levels of margin do each of you have with your time and moral decisions? Identify ways you, your teammate, and the team as a whole can encourage more margin. Brainstorm specifics to help each other and your team create a margin of victory.

My GamePlan

_____

_____

_____

_____

_____

_____

_____

_____

Father, I know it's easy to get so busy that the important things in life get pushed to the back burner. Forgive me for running so hard with my time that I don't spend the time I should with You. Help me say no to some good things to make room for time with You. Help me to draw the line far from temptation and sin so I have distance between what I know to be right and wrong. Create positive margin to ensure victory on the field and in life. Amen.

32

SECONDHAND GLORY

WisdomWalks Principle
Reflect God's glory; don't steal it.

God is not interested in receiving secondhand glory from our activity.
HENRY BLACKABY

Growing up with two older brothers meant I *never* got anything new. Nothing! I was given secondhand items all the time, including clothes, sporting equipment, and toys. It was hand-me-down living at its best. Since there is no such thing as a *hand-me-up*, I never had the chance to return the favor. However, I do remember getting a few new pairs of socks, so I had that going for me. It felt like Christmas morning.

Secondhand stuff had already been passed through the hands of my brothers. They had worn out the knees of the pants, busted zippers on jackets, destroyed toy cars, and made holes in everything. But my big day did come. When I was eight years old, my dad bought me a brand-new blue lacrosse stick called an STX Sam. I never knew what new smelled like until that day. Each night, the lacrosse stick replaced my dog in my bed. That stick didn't leave my side for months. The best part of the whole deal was that my brothers didn't get the chance to get their dirty hands on it before I did. It was a glorious moment! The lacrosse stick glowed because it passed through my hands *first*—not second, or third! That experience marked me as a young athlete.

The basic concept of *second hand* is having a previous owner (i.e., brothers). Second hand can never be new. We clearly understand this principle when it comes to possessions and even when it comes to secondhand information. Secondhand information is never dependable and is usually given with caution, such as, "Not sure about this play, but the coach said it would work every time we run it."

But what does *second hand* mean when it comes to God? He doesn't want secondhand, passed-down glory. You know what I'm talking about—

taking credit for ourselves when God should be getting it. This can be subtle, quickly giving credit to God *after* we take the credit first. Of course, we're always "spiritual" enough to not keep the glory for good…just long enough to enjoy it.

The key, though, is to reflect His glory, not absorb it. *We need to be mirrors, not sponges.* When we compete, we should reflect God's glory—and He should see Himself. If we are sponges, we absorb His glory and rob Him of the glory due His name.

The Bible clearly shows that *God rejects all secondhand glory. He only receives firsthand glory.* Giving Him the glory goes beyond who should get the credit. Credit is done with the mouth. Glory is done with the heart. Glory is about honoring our Master with our best and worshipping Him with a pure heart. When we get it right and honor Him first, God will honor us. First Samuel 2:30 (HCSB) says, "I will honor those who honor Me, but those who despise Me will be disgraced."

As athletes, it's easy to take credit, because we're always getting it from teammates, coaches, and fans. *The world of sports is an environment of recognition, praise, credit, and glory.* Too many athletes and coaches become glory hounds instead of glory reflectors. Glory hounds compete for others—to impress and get recognition. They feed off their own successes.

Nehemiah 6:15–16 talks about a great leader who was not a glory hound but a glory reflector:

So the wall was completed on the twenty-fifth of Elul, in fifty-two days. When all our enemies heard this, all the surrounding nations were afraid and lost their self-confidence, because they realized that this task had been done with the help of our God.

If anyone in the Bible could have been a glory hound, it was Nehemiah. He rebuilt the wall—a significant feat—in fifty-two days! He did the unthinkable, even though everyone told him he would not succeed. But it's crystal clear how he did it—he didn't do it himself. This incredible task was accomplished by God, not Nehemiah! There lies the secret of greatness, saying, "God did it." Not, "I did it." As Psalm 115:1 (HCSB) says:

Not to us, LORD, not to us, but to Your name give glory because of Your faithful love, because of Your truth.

But that's hard for athletes to do. The classic move most Christian athletes make is, "I did it, and I want to give God credit." It's not about giving God credit. Our desire instead should be that everyone know it is *God* who did it. *The competition is about God, not about us and our athletic accomplishments.*

As an athlete or coach, you are doing something significant. As a follower of Christ, you are always doing something significant, because you reflect Him every time you compete.

What if you decided, right from the get-go, that the glory for everything you do will go to Jesus? The FCA Competitor's Creed states: "Let the competition begin. Let the glory be God's." So reflect God's glory; don't steal it. Our Father delights to see Himself in you when you compete. It doesn't get any better than that!

Be a GameChanger!

Live Intentionally. Maximize Relationships. Pass the Torch.

Live It

When have you given God firsthand glory? When do you find yourself giving Him secondhand glory? Explain.

Read Genesis 4:1–7. In this story of Cain and Abel, how does God reject secondhand glory? Why?

When competing, why is it easy to take the glory?

Maximize It

Read Psalm 96:7–8; Zechariah 4:6; 1 Corinthians 10:31. What do these verses say about giving God glory? About it being a heart issue?

Do you find yourself being a glory hound or a glory reflector? (Be honest.) Why is it so easy to say "I did it" as an athlete? What prevents you from saying "God did it"?

How does Nehemiah's example inspire you as an athlete? What are some practical ways you can give God the glory first?

Pass It

Grab a teammate and discuss the *WisdomWalks* principle: *Reflect God's glory; don't steal it.* Talk about how each of you can better reflect God's glory. How might nurturing a team of glory reflectors change your team's chemistry?

My GamePlan

_____

_____

_____

_____

_____

_____

_____

_____

Lord, I admit it—I'm a glory hound. Forgive me. Help me, Lord, to not give You secondhand glory. I know You want firsts, not seconds. Teach me how to give You the glory, all the time. My goal is to be a glory reflector so You might be pleased to see Yourself in me. When I compete, I don't want to steal any glory from You. I want to be Your mirror, Father. In Jesus' name, amen.

33

THE SCOREBOARD

WisdomWalks Principle
Becoming more like Jesus is winning.

If winning isn't everything, why do they keep score?
VINCE LOMBARDI

Known as "The Flying Scotsman," Eric Liddell ran to victory in the 1924 Paris Olympics. He won a gold medal for Scotland in the 400 meters, set a new world record with his time of 47.6 seconds, and won a bronze in the 200-meter race. He was an amazing athlete who was not only a runner but also a rugby player and a missionary to China.

Liddell ran, spoke, and lived with incredible faithfulness. He never wavered from his commitment to Jesus Christ. The classic movie *Chariots of Fire* shows just how much of an impact Liddell made by living out his convictions. He once said, "We are all missionaries. Wherever we go we either bring people nearer to Christ or we repel them from Christ." While competing, his goal was to draw his peers to Christ by doing the little things like shaking the hands of other runners before each race. At the time, runners ran on cinder tracks. Liddell would offer his trowel (a small shovel) to fellow runners who had trouble digging their starting holes. Even though he was known as "The Flying Scotsman," he could as easily have been called "The Serving Scotsman."

He was always thinking about how he could glorify Christ in all he did. When others looked down on other competitors because they were different, he would come alongside those people and encourage them. His life was defined by his desire to please God in his competition. After competing, he went to China as a missionary, where he taught children in school, worked with extremely poor people, and rescued victims of war. Whatever he did, his goal was to become like Jesus. He lived out Jesus' words in John 15:16 by producing eternal results for the Lord:

You did not choose me, but I chose you and appointed you to go and bear fruit—fruit that will last. Then the Father will give you whatever you ask in my name.

For Liddell, winning wasn't the scoreboard, medals, records or awards, because he had a different definition of winning. In the world of sports, winning becomes the ultimate goal; and as a result, competitors adopt a mentality of winning at all costs. Winning consumes us and prevents us from seeing competition correctly. We view the opponent as the enemy who needs to be beat, destroyed, and annihilated. But I don't think Jesus would play sports with that concept. He was clear how we should respond to our enemies: " 'Love the Lord your God with all your heart and with all your soul and with all your strength and with all your mind' and, 'Love your neighbor as yourself' " (John 10:27).

Winning Jesus' way would be to compete in such a godly way that we elevate the level of everyone's play so that even the competitor gets better. *When Jesus commands us to love one another, that includes our neighbor— even the opposing team on game day!*

There are two possible definitions of *competition*. One is to defeat an opponent in score, skill, or combat. The other is defined by looking at the Latin word for competition, which is *competere*. The root word *com* means "with," not "against." This definition means "to walk alongside of, for two or more to work together to bring another along, or to partner." The second is a vastly different way to play sports. *The Christian view of competition could be defined as elevating each other's involvement to higher levels of participation, skill development, and effectiveness through a sport for the glory of God.*

There is nothing wrong with wanting to win. Winning is not the issue, but rather how we define it. If you define winning by the score, then your scoreboard is getting more points. However, if you define winning by glorifying God, then your scoreboard is becoming more like Jesus in competition. In *Chariots of Fire*, there is a scene in which Eric Liddell is talking to his sister, Jenny, about his decision to run now and become a missionary later. He says, "God has made me fast. When I run, I can feel His pleasure, and to run and win is to honor Him."

When we sense and feel God's pleasure in us while we compete, the scoreboard changes. When we desire to come alongside our competition and see them improve, we have redefined winning. When we release all our talents, skills, and gifts for God's glory, our opponents will see Jesus while we compete. We become the hands and feet of Jesus.

God used Liddell in a significant way because he was willing to keep his eyes fixed on Jesus and not on himself. As a result, he could focus on those around him. As an athlete, it's hard not to buy into the world's definition of winning. Becoming Christlike *while we compete* is the win.

Jesus has "appointed you to go and bear fruit—fruit that will last" (John 15:16). Winning is becoming more like Jesus.

Be a GameChanger!

Live Intentionally. Maximize Relationships. Pass the Torch.

Live It

If you had been one of the competitors running against Eric Liddell, how would you have responded to him? What kind of athlete are you in the heat of competition? Do people like playing with you or against you? Explain.

What are some examples of athletes and coaches winning at all costs? How has this impacted the sports world?

Read Galatians 5:16, 22–23; 1 John 2:3, 6. How do you act when you win? When you lose? How will these verses influence your perspective for future wins and losses?

Maximize It

What are some simple, practical ways you can implement the Christian definition of competition by coming alongside and elevating each other's play to the glory of God?

What "fruit" can God produce if you focus on winning His way?

Read Ephesians 4:11–16. As an athlete, what does it mean to become mature in Christ?

Pass It

Grab a teammate and discuss the *WisdomWalks* principle: *Winning is becoming more like Jesus.* How can this principle change the way you and your teammate compete? How can it change your team as a whole?

My GamePlan

_____

_____

_____

_____

_____

_____

_____

_____

_____

Lord, help me be an athlete who understands how to love others, even my opponents. I admit it's hard to love those I'm competing against, so teach me how to do it. Show me practical ways to come alongside them. I want to become more like Jesus every time I compete. May my talents and abilities be used for Your glory. In Jesus' name, amen.

34

WATER BOY

WisdomWalks Principle
If you want to be great, serve everybody.

Greatness is not found in possessions, power, position, or prestige.
It is discovered in goodness, humility, service, and character.
WILLIAM ARTHUR WARD

This summer I experienced one of the most intense athletic weekends of my life. Thankfully, I was only a spectator. But my oldest son was on the field in the middle of the challenge. The weekend was an FCA camp for team captains only, and it attracted some of the best athletes I've seen in one place, representing almost every major sport—from football to softball to track. For forty-eight hours, these young athletes were pushed to their mental, physical, emotional, and spiritual limits. They competed as teams in everything from football power-sled relays to tire flips to the tug-of-war. They ran relay sprints, played ultimate Frisbee, and even swam relays in the pool. There was virtually no break in the action and very little sleep. As the sun beat down and caused temperatures of over 100 degrees, I was exhausted just watching.

My job was simple. I was the "water boy." Along with a handful of other professional staff, I kept a close watch on the competitors to make sure they were staying hydrated. Trainers took care of minor injuries and looked for signs of heat exhaustion and dehydration. The competitors held up amazingly well. We set up two Water Boy Sports Hydration Systems where eight competitors at a time could get the water they needed to stay in the game. This "small job" of providing water became really important as the days and heat wore on.

When I was a high school athlete, the water boys were usually the butt of a lot of jokes. They did the job no one else wanted to do; they served the needs of those actually good enough to make the team. They never took a shot, ran a race, or scored a goal, but they still served. Yet they were often treated as the "least" important part of the team.

But Jesus never views those who play a seemingly "small" role as unimportant. He never looked down on those who served behind the scenes or did jobs nobody else wanted. In fact, Jesus flips that concept on its head. He says the least among us will be the greatest. Those we consider great—the best players, the best coaches—will only be considered great in God's eyes if they serve like the water boy serves.

If you want to be great, you have to serve. We are often just like the disciples. We want to be great. We want to be the star. We want to have all the attention. In Mark 9:33–37, the disciples were arguing with each other about who was the greatest. Can you imagine? Jesus, the picture and essence of greatness, was right there with them, showing them how to be great, and all they cared about was "who's number one?" So Jesus called them all over and confronted them. "If anyone wants to be first, he must be the very last, and the servant of all." Wow. Convicting, right? You'd think that would have ended the discussion. But shortly after that, the issue arose again. James and John, brothers, still didn't get it. They felt entitled to some preferential treatment. So they brought their mom along when they asked to sit on the left and right of Jesus in glory. So Jesus answers one more time.

Whoever wants to become great among you must be your servant, and whoever wants to be first must be slave of all. For even the Son of Man did not come to be served, but to serve, and to give his life as a ransom for many.

MARK 10:43–45

Jesus washes His disciples' feet. In John 13, Jesus shows us how to serve with humility, just as a water boy does. It was an expression and an example of genuine love.

[Jesus] got up from the meal, took off his outer clothing, and wrapped a towel around his waist. After that, he poured water into a basin and began to wash his disciples' feet, drying them with the towel that was wrapped around him…. "Now that I, your Lord and Teacher, have washed your feet, you also should wash one another's feet. I have set you an example that you should do as I have done for you."

VERSES 4–5, 14–15

Jesus came to serve out of the position of humility, not to sit in the place of honor. He didn't seek status; He served. Those whom we think are least important, God considers the most important.

Jesus gives us living water. Not only did He humble Himself and serve His disciples by washing their feet, not only did He serve us by exchanging His life for our freedom, but He also serves us daily by giving us living water. In John 4:10, Jesus answered [the Samaritan woman], "If you knew the gift of God and who it is that asks you for a drink, you would have asked him and he would have given you living water." Jesus gives us water that cleanses us from sin and satisfies our souls. That's better than even a cold glass of water on a scorching hot day!

We say all the time that we want to be more like Jesus. But when's the last time you heard someone say they want to be "the least"? Well, that's what Jesus became—the least. He served us and continues to serve us. Serving out of humility produces greatness. There is no other road to greatness. If you want to be great, serve everybody.

Be a GameChanger!

Live Intentionally. Maximize Relationships. Pass the Torch.

Live It

Is it easier for you to serve or be served? Why?

Which players and coaches on your teams would you identify as the best at serving? What do they do to serve?

Read Philippians 2:3–4. What is an essential quality of serving? What does it mean to make others more important than you?

Maximize It

Read Matthew 23:1–12; 1 Corinthians 1:27–29. How do these passages challenge your perception of what it takes to be the best or greatest?

What can you actively do to serve your teammates, coaches, and athletes? What are some ways to create a culture of humble serving?

Pass It

Grab a teammate and discuss the *WisdomWalks* principle: *If you want to be great, serve everybody.* What attitudes prevent a culture of serving from developing on your team? Brainstorm what you can do personally and as a team to serve each other and show appreciation for all who serve the team.

My GamePlan

_____

_____

_____

_____

_____

_____

_____

Father, I confess that serving others doesn't come naturally to me. But I realize that if I want to become great, I need to become more like Jesus. Thank You for modeling what it looks like to serve out of a heart of humility. Help me find specific ways to serve my teammates and coaches. And draw others to You by the way I serve. Amen.

35

GRIP IT AND RIP IT!

WisdomWalks Principle
Take a risk, and watch God make a play.

*God is looking for people through whom He can do the impossible—
what a pity that we plan only the things we can do ourselves.*

A. W. TOZER

When people ask me, "Are you a golfer?" I'm not sure how to answer. I like golfing, and I play the game, but I doubt you could classify me as a *golfer*. It's safer to say I'm an athlete who *tries* to play golf; it's a tough sport. I can have a great round and then a not-so-great round. Almost everyone who has teed off knows exactly what I'm talking about.

But the best round of golf I ever played was when a good friend gave me two pieces of advice—manage the course and "grip it and rip it." He told me to play to my strengths with absolute freedom and confidence. "Focus on what you do well on the course—clubs you use to hit with relative accuracy and consistency, not clubs you have little or no control over. Then, once you have your plan and have chosen the club, let it rip! If you're constantly thinking about the seven points of swing mechanics, or you're tentative with your swing, you'll never enjoy the game. That has to happen in practice, where bad habits can be corrected." So when I approached the ball, I said to myself, "Grip it and rip it!"

When athletes lack confidence, play timid, or aren't willing to take risks, they don't perform at their best. When you play not to lose, you lose. You feel pressure that kills performance. God wants us to play to win. Even though we'll make mistakes, playing with absolute confidence and freedom can also lead to a joy in competition that most athletes seldom experience.

The apostle Peter was the original "grip it and rip it" disciple. He was a spiritual risk taker with a heart and passion for Jesus even before he fully understood who Jesus was. He wanted to do great things and was willing to make mistakes along the way. Most people only remember his failures—

cutting off a man's ear in trying to defend Jesus, denying he knew Jesus out of fear, speaking before thinking, you name it. But Jesus saw Peter's courage, passion, energy, boldness, and faith.

> *"Lord, if it's you," Peter replied, "tell me to come to you on the water."*
>
> *"Come," He said.*
>
> *Then Peter got down out of the boat, walked on the water and came toward Jesus.*
>
> MATTHEW 14:28–29

All the disciples were afraid—the water was rough, it was dark, and they saw Jesus walking on the water. But Peter was the only one who took the risk to join Jesus on the water. Can you imagine the rush? And how his faith grew? We know that he sank, but he would never forget what he was capable of when he obeyed the voice of God.

Later on in the book of Acts, Peter risked speaking to large crowds about the resurrection, telling them to call on the name of Jesus for the forgiveness of sins and salvation. Not exactly an easy thing to do, especially when he was put in jail for doing so. But Peter was willing to take risks that stretched his own faith, that put what he believed to the test, and that required God to move in miraculous ways. Peter was not afraid to fail. As a result, he knew great victory—and also humbling defeat. Peter dared greatly and lived life to the full. And as he took risks, the Holy Spirit refined him in ways that prepared him to be courageously bold.

When we boldly take risks as God fills us and leads us, God does the miraculous in us and through us, too. In sports, the coach drives the culture. If the coach pulls players from the game to punish them every time they make mistakes, those players will play far below what they are capable of; they will never reach their full potential. If you fear making mistakes, you won't take advantage of opportunities when they present themselves. And everyone else on the team will play more tentatively as well. We like to say, "No risk, no reward. Know risk, know reward." If the coach gives players freedom to fail, they often get better fast. And they don't let mistakes crush them; they get right back in the game, saying, "Next time…I got this!"

The Bible is full of risk takers: Moses, Abraham, Gideon, David, Daniel,

Paul, Esther, Ruth, Mary…the list is endless. When God's people are filled with His Spirit, they have the courage to walk by faith. So don't be timid. Be bold. Get in the game. Grip it and rip it! Take a risk, and watch God make a play.

===⟨ **Be a GameChanger!** ⟩===

Live Intentionally. Maximize Relationships. Pass the Torch.

Live It

Read these words by former president Theodore Roosevelt:

> *It is not the critic who counts: not the man who points out how the strong man stumbles or where the doer of deeds could have done better. The credit belongs to the man who is actually in the arena, whose face is marred by dust and sweat and blood, who strives valiantly, who errs and comes up short again and again, because there is no effort without error or shortcoming, but who knows the great enthusiasms, the great devotions, who spends himself for a worthy cause; who, at the best, knows, in the end, the triumph of high achievement, and who, at the worst, if he fails, at least he fails while daring greatly, so that his place shall never be with those cold and timid souls who knew neither victory nor defeat.*

How does this quote speak to your heart? Does it make you want to get in the game and take some risks? Why or why not?

Maximize It

As coaches and competitors, what can we do to encourage freedom on the field and crush the fear of failure?

Read the story of Gideon in Judges 6–7, Esther in Esther 4–5, and Daniel in Daniel 2–6. What qualities did these people have in common? Why were they willing to take spiritual risks?

Pass It

Grab a teammate and discuss the *WisdomWalks* principle: *Take a risk, and watch God make a play.* What things prevent you from letting it rip on the field? What can you do personally and as team members to create a culture that encourages appropriate risk taking?

My GamePlan

_____

_____

_____

_____

_____

_____

_____

_____

_____

Father, I have a desire to be counted among the great spiritual risk takers like Peter and Ruth and Daniel. I want You to do great things in me and through me so I can be a difference maker. Fill me with Your Spirit so I may walk with courage and boldness. Take away my fear of failure and empower me to "grip it and rip it"—to attempt great things for You. Amen.

36

MARK OF EXCELLENCE

WisdomWalks Principle
Leave a God-mark, not a me-mark.

*Success means being the best. Excellence means being your best.
Success means exceeding the achievements of other people.
Excellence means matching your practice with your potential.*

BRIAN HARBOUR

After a hard workout session at an FCA Summer Sports Camp, one of the coaches challenged the campers to compete with excellence, because the kids were dragging through their second practice of the day. "Practice makes permanence," he said. "Perfect practice makes perfect."

"Practice makes perfect" is the way I've always heard it. But if you're practicing something wrong, it doesn't matter how many times you do it, it just makes it permanent, not perfect. The key is doing it right by doing it with excellence. Colossians 3:23 says, "Whatever you do, work at it with all your heart, as working for the Lord, not for men." The "whatever" part is hard, because it means pursuing excellence in all we do—including practice, lifting weights, training, eating, studying, and worshipping. God deserves our best, not our leftovers.

Excellence starts with the heart. Abraham Lincoln said it best: "I desire so to conduct the affairs of this administration that if, at the end, when I come to lay down the reins of power, I have lost every other friend on earth, I shall at least have one friend left, and that friend shall be down inside of me."

When you compete, what kind of mark do you want to leave? Are you pursuing excellence—or perfection? Edwin Bliss once said, "The pursuit of excellence is gratifying and healthy. The pursuit of perfection is frustrating, neurotic, and a terrible waste of time." If we want excellence as a competitor, we need to be athletes and coaches of excellence who are committed to pursuing excellence over the long haul. To achieve this, we must answer three questions:

1. *Who do you serve?* If your answer is "Jesus Christ," then also ask yourself, "Does He delight in my playing?" We say, "Without Christ we can do nothing," but we often do sports and life as if we can do something without Christ. Is it something or nothing? It has been said, "When I try, I fail. When I trust, He succeeds." We need to be on our guard for misplaced confidence.

2. *How's your work?* As an athlete, your work is your competition. Ephesians 2:10 says, "For we are God's worksmanship, created in Christ Jesus to do good works, which God prepared in advance for us to do." Doing the Lord's work with excellence and a faithful heart is the goal. Second Timothy 2:15 (HCSB) says: "Be diligent to present yourself approved to God, a worker who doesn't need to be ashamed, correctly teaching the word of truth." Are you an approved or an ashamed competitor? To stand approved, we need to serve with standards. We should be compelled to pursue excellence in all training, practicing, and playing.

But there's always an element of sacrifice involved. Michelangelo was only fourteen years old when he began training with Bertoldo de Giovanni, one of the greatest sculptors of his time. It was already obvious that this student was enormously gifted, and Bertoldo was wise enough to realize that gifted people are often tempted to coast rather than to grow. One day, when Michelangelo was toying with a sculpture far beneath his abilities, Bertoldo grabbed a hammer, stomped across the room, and smashed the work into thousands of pieces, shouting this unforgettable message: "Talent is cheap; dedication is costly!"

John Wooden said, "There is no substitute for hard work. Most people have a tendency to look for shortcuts or at least for the easiest way to complete any given task. If we only put out a minimum effort, we might get by in some situations, but in the long run, we won't fully develop the talents that lie within us." How is your competition? Is it excellent?

3. *What's your foundation?* If your answer is "the Word of God," then is the Word well used? As Christians, we need to have a passion for the Truth and to handle the Truth with accuracy. Titus 2:7 (HCSB) says, "Set an example of good works yourself, with integrity and dignity in your teaching." As we share with others, our examples need to be grounded in the Word of God—nothing more, nothing less.

Every time we serve and lead, we leave an imprint. But will it be a me-mark or a God-mark? When we're committed to excellence, we naturally desire to leave the kind of mark on others that will have an eternal impact. Being excellent requires the total release of our talents, gifts, and abilities to the calling of becoming more like Christ. We cannot hold back or keep anything for our own glory!

Martin Luther put it well, "The maid who sweeps her kitchen is doing the will of God just as much as the monk who prays—not because she may sing a Christian hymn as she sweeps but because God loves clean floors. The Christian shoemaker does his Christian duty not by putting little crosses on the shoes, but by making good shoes, because God is interested in good craftsmanship." Apply the same philosophy to the competitor, and it might be: "The Christian athlete or coach who competes is doing the will of God as much as the missionary who serves overseas—not because he or she gives God credit after winning a game but because God loves sportsmanship and a sport played with excellence."

What about you? Do you pursue excellence and making a God-mark? What kind of imprint are you leaving?

=======================〈 **Be a GameChanger!** 〉=======================

Live Intentionally. Maximize Relationships. Pass the Torch.

Live It

Why does excellence start with the heart? What does it mean to have an excellent heart before being an excellent competitor?

Do you think God is well pleased with your work? Why or why not? In what areas could you improve?

Maximize It

What does this statement mean to you? "The Christian competitor who competes is doing the will of God as much as the missionary who serves oversees—not because he or she gives God credit after winning a game but because God loves sportsmanship and a sport played with excellence."

Why is there always an element of sacrifice to anything that is excellent? What have you given up to pursue excellence as an athlete or coach?

Read Ecclesiastes 9:10; 1 Corinthians 10:31; 2 Corinthians 8:7; Philippians 1:9–10. What do these verses say about me-marks and God-marks? When are you tempted to leave a me-mark? Why?

Pass It

Grab a teammate and discuss the *WisdomWalks* principle: *Leave a God-mark, not a me-mark.* When have you left me-marks, and when have you left God-marks? What are some specific ways you can encourage your teammates and coaches to leave God-marks?

My GamePlan

_____

_____

_____

_____

_____

_____

_____

Lord, You are excellent. Show me how I can compete in such a way that people see excellence in all I do. I want them to talk about the power of Jesus, not my athletic accomplishments. I desire for the mark of Jesus to be all that is left. Amen.

37

THE RING

WisdomWalks Principle
Keep your eyes on the Prize.

Let us fix our eyes on Jesus, the author and perfecter of our faith.
HEBREWS 12:2

Tom Brady was coming off his third Super Bowl Championship and on top of the football world when, in June 2005, he was interviewed by *60 Minutes*. With three rings on his fingers and his name listed with the all-time great quarterbacks, you might think, *Here's a guy who has it all—fame, fortune, success*. But deep inside, Tom knew something was missing. He gave the viewers of the program a peek inside when he said, "Why do I have three Super Bowl rings and still think, *It's gotta be more than this.… This can't be what it's all cracked up to be*?" He had fulfilled his dreams yet was still empty.

I can relate. When I was growing up, I loved getting trophies. And by the time I finished high school, I had a case full of them. Some were more important to me than others. Three awards stood out the most—one was when I made the high school basketball all-tournament team; another was for being selected the academic athlete of the year; and the last one was for placing second in the punt, pass, and kick competition when I was twelve years old. I loved those awards and kept them for twenty years in a box in my basement. Even today, I enjoy getting a medal when I complete a triathlon, but they don't hold the same place in my heart.

In most professional sports today, it's all about the ring. Every sport at every level has a championship to play for. Sure, there's the Lombardi Trophy, the Stanley Cup, and even the Green Jacket, but everybody wants their own ring. Winning championships is the name of the game. Some say the ring serves as a status symbol and even personal validation. Players who dominate their sport are still questioned if they haven't won a championship—if they don't have a ring. They will even leave their current team to try to find the best opportunity to win a championship. Coach Vince Lombardi once said, "Winning isn't everything. It's the only thing." And many players today agree.

Wanting to win isn't a bad thing. But when the pursuit of "the ring" becomes the ultimate thing, we've got a problem. The apostle Paul puts it this way:

> *Do you not know that in a race all the runners run, but only one gets the prize? Run in such a way as to get the prize. Everyone who competes in the games goes into strict training. They do it to get a crown that will not last; but we do it to get a crown that will last forever.*
>
> 1 Corinthians 9:24–25

Paul, like any competitor, wanted to win. But he didn't want to chase just any old prize. He wanted to make sure it was the *right* prize—one that would be worth the effort and sacrifice. So Paul took a look back at all his accomplishments and did a Tom Brady: *"It's gotta be more than this."*

> *But whatever was to my profit I now consider loss for the sake of Christ. I consider them rubbish, that I may gain Christ and be found in Him. I press on toward the goal to win the prize for which God has called me heavenward in Christ Jesus.*
>
> Philippians 3:7–8, 14 abridged

In fact, Paul knew his box full of trophies was worth nothing compared to knowing Jesus. The forgiveness and freedom he experienced because of the sacrifice of Christ was better than anything he could earn himself. And his "rings" couldn't satisfy him like eternal life would.

Winning is temporary. The glory fades. We look to the ring to make us feel important and successful. And many of us get our identity from the things we accomplish. But God never designed the "rings" in our lives to satisfy us or give us our identity. When we put all our energy and passion into chasing rings or success or records, we will be disappointed and empty.

We've got to compete for the right prize. Jesus is the only prize that satisfies. He's the only thing worth pursuing with our whole heart. When we know Christ and experience His love, we are satisfied. We feel full and complete.

And I promise you'll never think, *It's gotta be more than this.*

So stop chasing after the rings of temporary pleasure and success. Stop searching for substitutes that will never satisfy. Keep your eyes on the Prize.

Be a GameChanger!

Live Intentionally. Maximize Relationships. Pass the Torch.

Live It

Do you want to win more than you want to know Jesus? Why or why not?

What "rings" are you pursuing? Explain.

Maximize It

Read Matthew 6:19–21. What does this passage say about desiring and pursuing treasure or "rings" in this life?

Evaluate your priorities. What are the most important things in your life—the things you desire and pursue with the most energy, time, and passion?
- What will last forever? What will only last in this life?
- What will be here today and gone tomorrow?

What priorities need to get rearranged around eternal values?

Read Matthew 5:6; Philippians 1:21. How do these passages reorient your focus for sports and life?

Pass It

Grab a teammate and discuss the *WisdomWalks* principle: *Keep your eyes on the Prize.* Talk about the things you're pursuing that are most important to each of you. Which only satisfy for a short time? Which have lasting value? Pray that every member of your team would reorder the priorities of their hearts around the prize of Christ.

My GamePlan

_____

_____

_____

_____

_____

_____

_____

_____

_____

Father, I pray that You will change my heart to love and pursue things that will last forever. Reorder my priorities and efforts so I put first things first. I know that worldly success looks good from the outside but leaves me empty on the inside. Help me to recognize the cheap substitutes that I desire and to refocus on Jesus, the only prize that satisfies. Amen.

38

HAY IN THE BARN

WisdomWalks Principle

Your tomorrow depends on your today.

My son, if you accept my words and store up my commands within you…
then you will understand the fear of the LORD
and discover the knowledge of God.

PROVERBS 2:1, 5 (HCSB)

The day before the Kansas City marathon, I met with Chris Anderson, our national director of FCA's Endurance Ministry. I was fired up for the race but a bit anxious about trying to run a personal record (PR). As I reflected on my training leading up to the race, I mentioned that I wished I'd done more long runs, more speed work, more conditioning, more everything. I was feeling the pressure.

He smiled really big and leaned across the table. "Dan, at this point, the hay is in the barn. The race is tomorrow. Nothing you can do now." Focused on the race and not fully understanding his point, I thought to myself, *I don't have hay or a barn.* He must have sensed my confusion, for he explained it meant the work had already been done and there was no more time to cram. The formal training was over and there was no looking back—nothing more to do but execute on race day. Now I just had to use what was stored up and let it work itself out during the race.

The next day, I thought about using my hay and the investment I'd made over the months leading up to the race. The days I didn't feel like getting in the twenty-mile training runs but did anyway were paying big dividends. As I cranked away in the last two miles, I began to pull away from the group I'd been running with the entire race. I immediately thought back to the year before, when my pack had left me in the dust as a result of my lackluster training. There had been no hay in the barn when I'd needed it. But this year was different. There was plenty of hay in the barn, and I was blessed with a PR. I ran well on race day because I trained hard months before. My preparation and practice impacted my future outcome.

Hay in the barn *is a powerful principle in every area of life—especially our spiritual lives.* Spiritually, the hay is the Word of God, and the barn is our heart. Sometimes, however, we fall into the trap of wanting a spiritual PR without putting in the spiritual investment. I admit it—sometimes I want God to show up and do something miraculous without my having to invest the time to know Him better. We think God will do His miraculous thing anyway, so what does it matter if we press in and get serious about our walk? If we love Jesus more, does that change anything? And what does it even look like to love God more? If we connect with Him daily and rely on Him to direct us throughout the day, will it really make a difference?

Proverbs 2:1 says to store up His commands. We must dive into the Word so our lives can be governed by truth and motivated by love. For me, *spending daily time in the Word is more about the future than today.* Yes, I draw on His Word daily, but when it comes to my training times, it always comes back to what I invested months earlier.

I will never regret spending "too much" time with Jesus. My mind-set has changed over the years. I used to think my devotions were all about *me*—what I got out of it and how much I needed it. Now I realize that God longs for me to commune with Him. My Father delights when His child posts up each day. He especially loves it when I linger longer in His presence. Stopping the rush of the day and being consumed by His love is essential. To worship daily is nonnegotiable for me.

Too many people skim—going through the motions. They say, "I wish I could spend more time in the Word, but…" We all have our reasons, but not one of them is a good one. No spiritual investment made for long-term impact. It becomes a matter of getting through today, not thinking about tomorrow. Then running on spiritual fumes becomes the norm.

How much spiritual hay is in the barn of your heart? Have you put in the time? Are you expecting great things with no spiritual sweat? Then let me ask you, "Would you make varsity without ever picking up the ball?" Or, "At mile twenty-four, what would you have left in the tank?"

Carve out the time. Make an investment. Go deeper. Start putting spiritual hay in the barn today. Your tomorrow depends on it.

Be a GameChanger!

Live Intentionally. Maximize Relationships. Pass the Torch.

Live It

How much preparation and practice do you put in for your sport? What impact does this have on you—and your team?

Do you find it hard to set aside time to spend in God's Word? If so, for what reasons? How might you begin to put more spiritual hay in your barn on a daily basis?

How do you make sure you don't fall into a rut when you spend time daily with the Lord? If you recognize that your tomorrow depends on your today, how does that impact your time with God?

Read Deuteronomy 5:29; John 14:21; Hebrews 6:1; 1 John 3:22. What do these verses say about spiritual hunger, spending time with God, and the benefits? How might you rearrange life to make God a priority?

Maximize It

Why does your tomorrow depend on today? Why is this true both on the field of competition and in your heart?

Read Daniel 6:1–12. How did Daniel prepare months before being thrown into the lions' den? Look at verse 10. How did his spiritual investment impact his outlook?

When problems have come into your own life, how has storing up God's commands from His Word helped? How might investing even more time pay spiritual dividends?

Pass It

Grab a teammate and discuss the *WisdomWalks* principle: *Your tomorrow depends on your today.* How might your physical and spiritual preparation impact your team? How different would your team be if everyone followed this principle?

My GamePlan

_____

_____

_____

_____

_____

_____

_____

_____

_____

Father, I desire to store Your commands inside me so I understand the fear of the Lord and discover the knowledge of God. I want to put spiritual hay in my heart today so I can be stronger tomorrow. I commit to pursue You, Lord—to linger a little longer in Your presence so I hear from You. Help me to go deeper in my walk with You. In Your name I pray, amen.

39

TRIPLE THREAT

WisdomWalks Principle
Be a spiritual threat.

Let's live our lives in such a way that when our feet hit the floor in the morning, Satan shudders and says, "Oh, no...they're awake!"

UNKNOWN

I still remember being a twelve-year-old aspiring basketball player and hearing NBA Hall of Famer Adrian Dantley teach about basketball's "triple threat." I learned that when you first receive the ball, you are in a great position with three potential options: dribble, shoot, or pass. I wouldn't soon forget the power of the triple threat. It changed the way I played basketball, and it even helped me beat my older brother in one-on-one a few times.

As followers of Christ, we also have a "triple threat." Our opponent, Satan, wants to defeat us and take us out. He doesn't want us to win and is working overtime to make sure you and I are discouraged and over-whelmed. We start believing that the sole goal in life is to survive—just get through one more day.

But *as competitors for Christ, we need to be a spiritual threat.* When I coach, I always tell players that they need to be a threat. I tell them, "If you get the ball and the defender knows you aren't going to do anything with it, the defender will smother you. But if the other players know you are a threat, they'll be on their heels when you have the ball." It changes every-thing about the game! In 1 Thessalonians 5:16–18, Paul gives us a great spiritual triple threat:

> *Be joyful always; pray continually; give thanks in all circumstances, for this is God's will for you in Christ Jesus.*

The threat is simply this: BE, PRAY, GIVE. This kind of triple threat will surely put Satan on his heels!

Threat No. 1: Be joyful always. It would have been easier to live it out if Paul had written, "Be joyful," not, "Be joyful always." *Always* seems impossible; *sometimes* is more realistic. But his command instructs us to be full of joy all the time: "You *will* do life with joy in your heart—*all the time*—you got it?" Joy is more than happiness; it's at the core of our soul. Joy is internal, and happiness is external. Happiness can come and go, but joy is here to stay. In John 15:11, Jesus said, "I have told you this so that my joy may be in you and that your joy may be complete." That means His joy should fill up our hearts so that the world outside has no room. A good friend once challenged me with this thought (he knew I was influenced too much by the outside stuff): "Don't let anyone or anything rob you of the joy God has placed in you." We should experience joy whether we win or lose.

Do you have joy in your life? Do others see it? Joy should overflow—gush out of your life. Then you will be a threat to Satan and influence others for Christ.

Threat No. 2: Pray continually. As if instructing us to pray wasn't hard enough, Paul had to tack on that extreme word *continually.* You might be thinking, *I pray, just not all the time.* But Paul says we should *always* be connected to our Maker. A prayer should *always* be in our hearts and on our lips. Many times we just pray when we need something—like a big win against a tough team. A couple of prayer principles have radically changed my life.

First, *prayer is not telling God what He already knows, but God revealing to us what we do not know.* Our goal is not to give God a report through our prayer. Trust me, God does not need to be updated. What He wants is for us to dig deep and find out what is below the surface. Prayer should be a discovery time, not a reporting time. Praying should be a workout.

Second, *prayer changes us the most.* Instead of praying for God to do something, we should ask God to reveal Himself to us. Prayer is a way of following hard after God. It should change the way we live. E. M. Bounds said, "Get people to pray, and they will stop sinning, because prayer creates a distaste for sinning." Are your prayers making Satan nervous?

Threat No. 3: Give thanks in all circumstances. In all three threats, Paul uses extreme commands. First it was "always," then "continually," and, finally, "all." Just as Ephesians 4:29 says, we need to use our words to build up others. When we speak, we speak either life or death. Giving thanks means speaking life in every situation: in the locker room, classroom, home, on the phone, and even in our text messaging. Proverbs 12:18 says that reckless words pierce like a sword, but the tongue of the wise brings healing. When you speak, do you bring healing? Is Satan threatened by the way you talk? Does he fear every time you open your mouth because he knows you are speaking blessing and thanksgiving?

The triple threat is simple: BE, PRAY, GIVE. Your teammates are depending on you to be joyful, pray continually, and give thanks. What are you waiting for? Be a spiritual threat!

Be a GameChanger!

Live Intentionally. Maximize Relationships. Pass the Torch.

Live It

Would you say that you are a threat to Satan? Why or why not?

Out of the three threats, which one are you doing best? Which one do you need to work on most?

Read Psalm 63:8; Proverbs 12:18; 18:21; 28:14–28; John 15:11; 2 Corinthians 11:28–29; Ephesians 4:29. What do these verses say about the reason for, and the benefits of, being a triple threat?

Maximize It

As a competitor, how can you be a triple threat when you compete? Give an example of each threat.

How can the triple threat concept change your life both on and off the field? How can it change others as you become a triple threat?

Reread 1 Thessalonians 5:16–23. What is the end result of BE, PRAY, GIVE? How can this impact the way you compete?

Pass It

Grab a teammate and discuss the *WisdomWalks* principle: *Be a spiritual threat.* How can you experience joy as a team? How can you pray continually? Give thanks always? How would joy, prayer, and thanks change the culture of your team in the locker room and on the field?

My GamePlan

_____

_____

_____

_____

_____

_____

_____

Lord, my goal is clear. My mission is set: Be. Pray. Give. That is what I desire. Help me to be a spiritual threat. I desire not only to have that transformation happen in my life, but also that I be able to transfer that impact to others. I long to be joyful, pray continually, and give thanks. Teach me, Jesus, to be the triple threat You know I can be. Thank You, Father, for hearing my prayers today. I will trust in Your work, Your way. Amen.

40

WHO DO YOU PLAY FOR?

WisdomWalks Principle
Play for the name on the front, not the back.

*Moses said to God, "Suppose I go to the Israelites and say to them,
'The God of your fathers has sent me to you,'
and they ask me, 'What is his name?' Then what shall I tell them?"
God said to Moses, "I AM WHO I AM.
This is what you are to say to the Israelites: 'I AM has sent me to you.'"*

EXODUS 3:13–14

The University of Maryland became the first college football team fifty years ago to have the players' names sewn on their jerseys. And this past year, their new head coach, Randy Edsall, thought it was time to go back to the good ol' days by removing the names. "I'm just a firm believer that you play for what's on the front of the jersey. When we're long gone, our school's name is still going to be here, and that's what it's all about," he said. Some of the most successful sports teams, like the New York Yankees, have never had individual names on their jerseys. The army football team had "West Point" stitched on the back instead of the players' names; they represented something bigger than themselves.

When Herb Brooks, coach of the 1980 US Olympic hockey team that beat the Soviets and went on to win the gold, was asked what he wanted on his tombstone, he said, "It's about the name on the front of the jersey, not the name on the back." He knew that the team was more important than the individual. And he wanted everyone to know who he was coaching for and who the players were playing for. It was an honor to play for the United States of America.

As we coach and compete, we need to remember who we play for and who we represent. It's easy to forget. We get our own egos mixed up in our mission. But the team name is bigger than our name, and when we put on that jersey, we represent that name.

However, there is a name even bigger than our team name. That name is Jesus, and we represent Him above all else.

In John 8, the Jews were questioning Jesus about who He was. Jesus responded by saying, "Before Abraham was born, I am!" (verse 58). In other words, Jesus gave them His name—I AM. That's the same name God told Moses in Exodus 3:14. Jesus is God the Son. And in the book of John, Jesus gives us seven dimensions of His name, which all portray a clear picture of who we play for, and who we live for.

I am the Bread of life. In John 6:35, Jesus refers to God's provision of manna from heaven and water from a rock to His people as they wandered in the wilderness for forty years. Without it, the Israelites would have perished. Jesus is the true Bread of life. Those who come to Him will never go hungry; those who believe will never be thirsty.

I am the Light of the world. In John 8:12, Jesus promises we will never walk in darkness. He has overcome evil. His Word is a lamp for our feet and a light for our path. He calls us to follow Him; we can trust His direction for our lives.

I am the Gate for the sheep. In John 10:7, Jesus tells us that He is the gate that leads to safety. The thief wants to steal the sheep, but Jesus is the gate by which the sheep would enter to be saved. Once we are saved, we have freedom and abundant life.

I am the Good Shepherd. In John 10:11, 27–30, Jesus makes it personal. He says He knows us, and we know Him. He takes care of us and protects us. When He calls, we recognize His voice and follow Him. He even lays down His life for us.

I am the Resurrection and the Life. In John 11:25–26, Jesus flashes forward to His own resurrection that will conquer sin and death once and for all. When He rises from the dead and appears to His followers, He sparks a movement of believers who cannot help but tell everyone what they have seen and heard!

I am the Way, the Truth, and the Life. In John 14:6, Jesus makes it clear that He is the only path to eternal life. No one comes to the Father except through Jesus. There are many paths that may lead to a good life, but only one leads to eternal life.

I am the True Vine. In John 15:5, Jesus tells us He is the very source of our life. We must seek Him and remain in constant connection with Him.

Otherwise, we can do nothing. Our life will not bear fruit that lasts.

As competitors and coaches, we play for Jesus. We compete for the One who is our very life. He gives us food and drink that satisfies our soul—that gives us peace, value, and assurance. His Word gives us wisdom for every challenge or crossroads we face. He lights our path so we know the way to go and can avoid things that could trip us up. He speaks to us—and when we listen, we hear His voice. When we hit the gym or take the field, when we enter the arena, on and off the field, we play for Jesus. Sometimes we forget this and play for ourselves—our recognition, our future, our glory. We become prideful and want to "take the podium" in victory. But there is no room for pride or selfishness as a Christian who competes. In humility, we need to accept responsibility and give credit to others. At the end of the day, we need to represent His name well. Others should see something different in us. It's not about you or me; it's about Him. When we put on our jersey, the name on the front of our jersey is JESUS. And *we play for the name on the front, not the back!*

Be a GameChanger!

Live Intentionally. Maximize Relationships. Pass the Torch.

Live It

As a competitor or coach, what motivates you? Do you care more about your personal success or the success of the team? Explain.

With so many athletes today pointing to the name on the back of their jersey after a big play, how can you turn the tide on your team?

Maximize It

Read Galatians 1:10–11. As a Christian competitor, are you competing to please God or people? How would others be able to tell from your actions?

Read 1 Samuel 16:6–7; 2 Chronicles 16:9. What is God looking for when He identifies people to lead and serve? Why is the heart really the most important thing?

Pass It

Grab a teammate and discuss the *WisdomWalks* principle: *Play for the name on the front, not the back.* How can you actively demonstrate this principle to team members? When other teammates play for themselves, how does this affect the team? Talk with coaches and teammates about what it means to play for Jesus.

My GamePlan

_____

_____

_____

_____

_____

_____

_____

_____

_____

Father, thank You for the opportunity to play and compete for the name on the front of my jersey—the name of Jesus. Help me remember that I represent You with my words, my attitudes, my effort, and my actions! Hold me to a higher standard so that I demonstrate what it looks like to be a great teammate. Amen.

LUST PATROL

WisdomWalks Principle
Sin never delivers what it promises.

He that but looketh on a plate of ham and eggs to lust after it hath already committed breakfast with it in his heart.

C. S. LEWIS

The late Paul Harvey once told the story of how an Eskimo attracts—and then kills—a wolf. The Eskimo coats a knife blade with animal blood, allows it to freeze, then adds layers until the knife is completely concealed. Then he fixes the knife in the ground with the blade up. When a wolf follows his sensitive nose to the scent, he begins licking the knife, tasting the frozen blood. He begins to lick faster, more and more vigorously, lapping the blade until the keen edge is bare. So great becomes his craving for blood that the wolf does not notice the razor-sharp sting of the naked blade on his own tongue, nor does he recognize the instant at which his insatiable thirst is being satisfied by his own warm blood. His carnivorous appetite just craves more—until the dawn finds him dead in the arctic snow.

It's a poignant picture of what lust can do—it can feverishly consume us!

But I've never once heard someone admit, "When it comes right down to it, I'm lustful." Have you?

That's because you can't see lust in the mirror. It's so easy to hide. We disguise it with words like *desire, passion,* and *ambition.* Lust is often associated with sex. But the concept of lust can be applied to almost every area of life. There can be athletic lust, intellectual lust, spiritual lust, and fitness lust, to name a few.

As competitors, we understand the law of the harvest. What we sow or plant today won't produce results today, or even tomorrow, but will produce great results down the road. For example, in basketball, working overtime on shooting will produce not just a better shooter, but a better player for the team. *The law of the harvest is about later and greater.* It always delivers. You can count on it.

But *the law of lust is about the "now" and the "foul."* It never delivers what it promises. Lust says that you can have anything instantly and that it will satisfy. It tempts us to do anything to get it, regardless of the consequences. However, the "you can have it now" pleasure is short-lived, and committing the foul perverts the original purpose. For example, sexual lust violates love and says, "I want it now, regardless of who I hurt or abuse in the process, including myself." Lust takes what God has made for good pleasure and distorts it.

Most honest competitors will admit they battle with athletic lust—wanting the results without the time and commitment of training. We want the starting position on the team without the discipline. We want the spotlight on us. It's all about the *want* without the *work*, and this attitude is everywhere in sports. Athletic lust destroys teams because it's based on selfishness.

There's an even more destructive kind of lust, however, that has nothing to do with athletics or sex. Lurking below the surface, tempting all followers of Christ, is spiritual lust. And just as we do with athletic lust, we expect results without effort. The desire is to be spiritually mature without any commitment.

Spiritual lust creates a one-sided relationship with Jesus Christ and places demands on God. It even creeps into our prayer life. We lust for answers that benefit us—answers that take care of our needs according to our wants and desires. We may not pray it this way, but God knows what we're thinking: *Lord, not THY will be done, but MY will be done.* Spiritual lust is consumed with "What can I get from God?" instead of "What can I give to Him?"

We need to be continually on lust patrol. We must proactively and intentionally patrol the perimeters of our hearts to make sure lust is not leaking into our souls. Lust leaves no peace or joy. It takes but never gives. It consumes but never satisfies. It drinks but never quenches your thirst. Paul warns us what happens when sin is planted in our hearts:

> *The one who sows to please his sinful nature, from that nature will reap destruction; the one who sows to please the Spirit, from the Spirit will reap eternal life.*

GALATIANS 6:8

We need to be willing to look in the mirror and call lust what it is. If athletes and coaches around the world would recognize it and ask Jesus for forgiveness, we could be freed of this sin that weighs us down in so many areas of life. Lust cripples us spiritually. It makes us spiritually weak.

Sin never delivers what it promises, but obedience does. Let's be athletes and coaches known for our obedience—known for pursuing holiness with every ounce of energy God has given us. If we do so, we can change the world of sports.

Be a GameChanger!

Live Intentionally. Maximize Relationships. Pass the Torch.

Live It

What challenged you the most about this WisdomWalk? What types of lust do you struggle with? Why?

Why is it so hard to see lust in the mirror?

In what specific ways can you patrol the perimeter of your soul?

Maximize It

Read Proverbs 7:6–27. This story describes how a young man falls into the trap of sexual sin. What can we learn from his fall?

Read Genesis 39:6–9. How did Joseph respond to sexual temptation? How is Joseph's response different than the young man's in Proverbs 7?

Have you experienced the law of the harvest in your sports or personal life? What did you learn from it? What do you need to change in your life so you can live by the law of the harvest and not the law of lust?

Read Psalm 126:5–6; Proverbs 11:18; Galatians 6:7–10; James 1:19–25. What do these Scriptures say about the pitfalls of lust and the benefits of obeying God? Confess to God the areas of lust you struggle with and ask Him to break the hold they have on you.

Pass It

Grab a teammate and discuss the *WisdomWalks* principle: *Sin never delivers what it promises.* Talk about how you can create a lust-free culture on your team. How important is it to keep your talk clean in the locker room? How can you help each other keep your eyes pure?

My GamePlan

_____

_____

_____

_____

_____

Father in heaven, I call upon Your name with boldness and power, asking for Your grace and mercy. I confess my lust in these areas of life: (list them). I am sorry. I ask for wisdom and revelation to take the steps necessary to live a victorious life. Place in me a desire for purity in every area of my life. Keep watch over my heart. May Your Holy Spirit fill me with Your strength. I ask for my life to be marked with the law of the harvest. I plant holiness and righteousness into my life, so that great things will spring forth at a later time because of my obedience today. Thank You, Jesus. Amen.

I am a Christian first and last.
I am created in the likeness of God Almighty to bring Him glory.
I am a member of Team Jesus Christ. I wear the colors of the cross.

I am a Competitor now and forever.
I am made to strive, to strain, to stretch, and to succeed in the arena of competition.
I am a Christian Competitor and as such, I face my challenger with the face of Christ.

I do not trust in myself.
I do not boast in my abilities or believe in my own strength.
I rely solely on the power of God.
I compete for the pleasure of my heavenly Father, the honor of Christ,
and the reputation of the Holy Spirit.

My attitude on and off the field is above reproach—my conduct beyond criticism.
Whether I am preparing, practicing, or playing,
I submit to God's authority and those He has put over me.
I respect my coaches, officials, teammates, and competitors out of respect for the Lord.

My body is a temple of Jesus Christ.
I protect it from within and without.
Nothing enters my body that does not honor the Living God.
My sweat is an offering to my Master. My soreness is a sacrifice to my Savior.

I give my all—all of the time.
I do not give up. I do not give in. I do not give out.
I am the Lord's warrior—a competitor by conviction and a disciple of determination.
I am confident beyond reason because my confidence lies in Christ.
The results of my efforts must result in His glory.

LET THE COMPETITION BEGIN.
LET THE GLORY BE GOD'S.

If this is the desire of your heart, then you are ready to join TEAM FCA.

www.fca.org

ACKNOWLEDGMENTS

Thanks to all the WisdomWalkers who turned *WisdomWalks* into a movement. It has been an amazing journey!

Thank to our wives: Dawn and Ivelisse; and to our kids, our daily reminders to stay on the path: Kallie, Abigail, and Elijah Britton; Jimmy, Jacob, John, and Grace Page.

Thanks to the hundreds of coaches, teammates, friends, staff, pastors, ministry partners, and family members who have invested in us; you have helped shape us into the men we are today and have played a significant part in the principles you will find in *WisdomWalks SPORTS*.

Deep appreciation to the all-star team at Summerside Press—Jason, Joanie, and Ramona—for your enthusiasm for *WisdomWalks SPORTS* and our shared passion for changing the world of sports.

The Fellowship of Christian Athletes is the most amazing ministry in the world. Special thanks to the entire FCA team: the men and women who walk with Jesus and faithfully invest in the next generation of athletes, coaches, and teams.

Thanks to our own Warriors, Watchmen, and Workmen. Without you, there wouldn't be *WisdomWalks*.

To our heavenly Father, for giving us Jesus,
the ultimate WisdomWalker, to show us the way,
the truth, and the life.

40 GAME-CHANGING PRINCIPLES

for Athletes, Coaches & Teams

1 In a single moment, God can change a heart.

2 We do the training; God does the changing.

3 Be the best you.

4 We're better together.

5 You can't fake the Almighty.

6 Think like a rookie; play like a pro.

7 Run with Jesus.

8 If you want to win, follow the Plan.

9 Don't worry; be praying.

10 You need to die to live.

11 Consistency leads to excellence.

12 If it's fun, it gets done.

13 Coaches love their players; players love each other.

14 Serving is leading.

15 Toxic material will make you sick.

16 Two are better than one.

17 If you don't fight, you're dead meat.

18 Engage God, no matter what.

19 Faith overcomes fear.

20 Humility unlocks greatness in others.

21 Character is formed in the fire.

22 Review your life film.

23 Speak life, not death.

24 Excuses lead to failure.

25 Depend on Him to shut down sin.

26 Prayer unleashes God's power.

27 Manage your energy for the winning edge.

28 God loves spiritual sweat.

29 Rest brings refreshment.

30 Impress at a distance; impact up close.

31 As the margin grows, victory is yours.

32 Reflect God's glory; don't steal it.

33 Becoming more like Jesus is winning.

34 If you want to be great, serve everybody.

35 Take a risk, and watch God make a play.

36 Leave a God-mark, not a me-mark.

37 Keep your eyes on the Prize.

38 Your tomorrow depends on your today.

39 Be a spiritual threat.

40 Play for the name on the front, not the back.

DAN BRITTON serves as the Fellowship of Christian Athletes' Executive Vice President of Ministry Programs at the National Support Center in Kansas City. He has been on FCA staff since 1991, first serving for thirteen years in Virginia. Dan oversees the ministry advancement, including Camps, Coaches Ministry, Campus Ministry, Community Ministry, Training, Digital Ministry, and Resource Development. While at St. Stephens High School in Virginia and at the University of Delaware, Dan was a standout lacrosse player. He continued his career by playing professional indoor lacrosse for four years with the Baltimore Thunder, earning a spot on the All-Star team, and was nominated by his teammates for both the Service and Unsung Hero awards. Dan is now a frequent speaker at schools, churches, conferences, camps, conventions, and retreats. He still plays and coaches lacrosse and even enjoys running marathons. He is married to Dawn, whom he met in youth group in eighth grade, and they reside in Overland Park, Kansas, with their three children: Kallie, Abby, and Elijah.

You can e-mail Dan at **dbritton@fca.org.**

Fellowship of Christian Athletes

Vision: To see the world impacted for Jesus Christ through the influence of athletes and coaches.

Mission: To present to athletes and coaches, and all whom they influence, the challenge and adventure of receiving Jesus Christ as Savior and Lord, serving Him in their relationships and in the fellowship of the church.

Values: Integrity • Serving • Teamwork • Excellence

About the Authors

JIMMY PAGE serves as a Vice President of Field Ministry and the National Director of the Health & Fitness ministry for the Fellowship of Christian Athletes. Growing up in the snow country of Rochester, New York, he became a three-sport athlete in high school and went on to graduate with two degrees from Virginia Tech. For nearly twenty years, he has been a leader in the medical fitness industry, operating wellness facilities affiliated with Sinai Hospital and Johns Hopkins. Jimmy is also a certified Nike-Sparq Trainer and currently hosts a daily radio segment and national podcast on iTunes called *Fit Life Today*, offering a blend of spiritual, mental, and physical health principles that promote abundant life. As a communicator, Jimmy is a frequent speaker at schools, churches, camps, and retreats and a trainer for corporate and nonprofit organizations, challenging people to transform their lives, walk with Jesus, and influence others. He has a contagious enthusiasm and passion for life. As a lifelong athlete, Jimmy enjoys coaching, cycling, and triathlons. He is married to his college sweetheart, Ivelisse, and they reside in Maryland with their four children: Jimmy, Jacob, John, and Gracie.

You can e-mail Jimmy at **jpage@fca.org.**

Impacting the World for Christ through Sports

Fellowship of Christian Athletes is the world's largest sports ministry, reaching over two million people each year. Since 1954, FCA has cultivated Christian principles in local communities nationwide by encouraging, equipping, and empowering others to serve as examples and make a difference.

Fellowship of Christian Athletes | 8701 Leeds Road | Kansas City, MO 64129
www.fca.org • 800-289-0909

Get the First WISDOMWALKS Book

A Playbook for a Life of Impact!

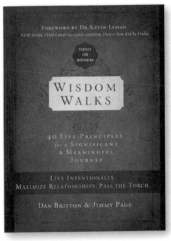

WisdomWalks is a real-life guide for walking purposefully with God and living the life of significance you were created for. Forty intentional, spiritual, life-changing connections will transform the way you think and do life. Each WisdomWalk features one key life principle, a real-life story, questions for individuals or groups, action steps, and lots more—all based on the truths and wisdom of God's Word.

Perfect for parents, coaches, and leaders to pass the torch to the next generation.

"A spiritual home run for personal growth, discipleship, and mentoring. Biblical, practical, inspiring, and digestible! I'm all in!"

CHIP INGRAM, Living on the Edge

"Dan and Jimmy didn't invent mentoring, just the mentoring game plan. I know these two FCA leaders personally, and you will be blessed by their powerful insights!"

JAMES B. "BUCK" MCCABE, CFO, Chick-fil-A, Inc.

192 Pages/5 x 7/Pearlescent Debossed Hardcover/Deluxe Slipcase
ISBN 978-1-935416-61-6
Available from your local retailer or at amazon.com,
barnesandnoble.com, and christianbook.com.

Join the weekly WisdomWalks e-newsletter.
Go to www.wisdomwalks.org to sign up.